The Child in the Family
Volume 11

The Monograph Series of the
International Association for Child
and Adolescent Psychiatry and
Allied Professions

Children and Violence

EDITED BY

COLETTE CHILAND, M.D., Ph.D.

J. GERALD YOUNG, M.D.

With editorial assistance and translation of the French
chapters by Diana Kaplan, Ph.D.

JASON ARONSON INC.
Northvale, New Jersey
London

This work was supported by a grant from the Medical Fellows Program of the Office of Mental Retardation and Developmental Disabilities, State of New York. Parts of Chapter 6 are reprinted from *The Psychological Effects of War and Violence on Children,* edited by L. Leavitt and N. Fox. Copyright © 1993 by Lawrence Erlbaum Associates and reprinted with permission.

This book was set in 11 point English Times by Lind Graphics of Upper Saddle River, New Jersey, and printed and bound by Haddon Craftsmen of Scranton, Pennsylvania.

Library of Congress Cataloging-in-Publication Data

Children and violence / edited by Colette Chiland, J. Gerald Young: with editorial assistance and translation of the French chapters by Diana Kaplan.
  p. cm. — (Child in the family: v. 11)
  Includes bibliographical references and index.
  ISBN 1-56821-235-6
  1. Children and violence. I. Chiland, Colette. II. Young, J. Gerald. III. Series.
  [DNLM: 1. Violence — in infancy & childhood. WS 350.8.A4 C5363 1994]
HQ784.V55C44   1994
303.6 — dc20
DNLM/DLC
for Library of Congress   94-3943

Manufactured in the United States of America. Jason Aronson Inc. offers books and cassettes. For information and catalog write to Jason Aronson Inc., 230 Livingston Street, Northvale, New Jersey 07647.

CONTRIBUTORS

Dora Black, M.B., FRC Psych DPM
Consultant
Child & Adolescent Psychiatry
Royal Free Hospital
Pond Street
Hampstead
London, NW3 20QG
England

Bob Blizzard
Medical Statistician
Royal Free Hospital Medical School
Pond Street
Hampstead
London, NW3 20QG
England

James R. Brasic, M.D., M.P.H.
Research Assistant Professor
of Psychiatry
Coordinator, Developmental
Neurobiology Unit
Division of Child and Adolescent
Psychiatry
New York University School of
Medicine
New York, N.Y. 10016
U.S.A.

Richard Maxwell Brown
Beekman Professor Emeritus of
Northwest and Pacific History
University of Oregon
Department of History
College of Arts and Sciences
175 Prince Lucien Campbell Hall
Eugene, Ore. 97403–1288
U.S.A.

Salvador Celia, M.D., Ph.D.
Leo Kanner Institute
Rua Dario Pederneiras 513
CEP 90610
Porto Alegre, RS, Brazil

Brandon S. Centerwall, M.D.,
M.P.H.
Assistant Professor
Department of Epidemiology, SC-36
School of Public Health and
Community Medicine
University of Washington
Seattle, Wash. 98195
U.S.A.

Colette Chiland, M.D., Ph.D.
Professor of Clinical Psychology
René Descartes University
Psychiatrist, Alfred Binet Center
75013 Paris
France

Yecheskiel Cohen, Ph.D.
Executive Director
B'nai B'rith Women Residential
Treatment Center
P.O. Box 16017
Bayit Vagan
Jerusalem 91160
Israel

Jean Harris Hendriks, F.R.C. Psych.
Consultant
Child and Adolescent Psychiatry
Royal Free Hospital
Pond Street
Hampstead
London, NW3 20QG
England

Tony Kaplan, M.B., C.h.B., M.R.C.
Psych.
Consultant, Child and Adolescent
Psychiatry
Royal Free Hospital Medical School
Pond Street
Hampstead
London, NW3 20QG
England

Marguerite E. Malakoff, Ph.D.
Department of Humanities and
Social Science
and Department of Psychology
Claremont Graduate School
Harvey Mudd College
Claremont, Calif. 91711
U.S.A.

Steven Marans, Ph.D.
Harris Assistant Professor of
Child Psychoanalysis
Yale University
Child Study Center
230 South Frontage Rd.
P.O. Box 3333
New Haven, Conn. 06510-8009
U.S.A.

Marie Rose Moro, M.D.
Associate Professor
University of Paris
12, rue Léon
F75018 Paris
France

Per-Anders Rydelius, M.D., Ph.D.
Professor and Chairman
Department of Child and
Adolescent Psychiatry
Karolinska Institutet
St. Goran's Children's Hospital
S-112 81 Stockholm
Sweden

Brian Sheitman, M.D.
Faculty Research Fellow
Division of Child and Adolescent
Psychiatry
New York University School of
Medicine
New York, N.Y. 10016
U.S.A.

Madeleine Studnick, M.D.
Faculty Research Fellow
Division of Child and Adolescent
Psychiatry
New York University School of
Medicine
New York, N.Y. 10016
U.S.A.

J. Gerald Young, M.D.
Professor of Psychiatry and
Director, Developmental
Neurobiology Unit
Division of Child and
Adolescent Psychiatry
New York University School of
Medicine
New York, N.Y. 10016
U.S.A.

PREFACE AND DEDICATION

Violence is a grim topic, particularly in relation to children, but the penalties for ignoring it are serious. Dr. Irving Philips, president of the International Association for Child and Adolescent Psychiatry and Allied Professions (IACAPAP), suggested the topic of children and violence for a volume to accompany and stimulate the scientific activities of the the 1994 Congress of IACAPAP in San Francisco. We were enthusiastic because it is a timely subject for such a book but concerned because the public seeks to turn aside from this unpleasant subject and might not want to see more of the facts in print. Dr. Philips was a man not easily turned aside from his goals by difficulties. He persisted, and we moved ahead with the preparation of this book, Volume XI in the Monograph Series of IACAPAP. His death in the summer of 1992 robbed us of a wise and thoughtful leader, but we are committed to continue his spirit of support for children. Fortunately, the energetic intelligence of our current president, Dr. Donald Cohen, has nurtured this book and carried forward the activities of IACAPAP.

Clinicians working with children might seem to be insulated from the world of violence even when children are not. Regrettably, clinicians do not always enjoy such safety from violence, as the recent death of our colleague Dr. Mahfoud Boucebci painfully demonstrated. Dr. Boucebci, a child and adolescent psychiatrist who was a vice president of IACAPAP, was murdered, stabbed in his car outside his hospital in Algiers on the morning of 15 June 1993. He not only cared for children struggling for their own survival in a troubled world but was outspoken about their needs. For this, he was murdered.

Dr. Philips and Dr. Boucebci were the essence of physicians, each offering the best of himself to the children who came to him for care. We dedicate this book to them in gratitude for their vision and dedication, which continue to guide us.

Colette Chiland
J. Gerald Young

INTRODUCTION

Much information is available concerning violence in the lives of children. The problem for the editors of a book on the subject is how to choose the topics to be included, necessarily neglecting other worthy subjects. Such obvious examples as a chapter providing the appalling statistics documenting the intrusion of violence into the world of children and a chapter describing our current knowledge about the physical and sexual abuse of children were not included because extensive literature on these subjects is readily available elsewhere; examining fresh topics seemed more likely to contribute to this dark field.

Quick answers may be quack answers in our search for the causes of violence. This book examines multiple factors influencing the lives of children at different levels: the family, the neighborhood, and the culture. As preparation for this discussion, we offer two chapters discussing violence from the perspectives of philosophy and psychology (Chiland) and the brain sciences (Young et al.).

The chapters in Part II examine the role of violence in the immediate world of the child: his or her family and home. We all accept that fundamental attitudes are molded within the family matrix of the childhood years, but are our judgments about these influences accurate? Is an event so devastating to an adult understanding, as when one parent kills the other (Kaplan et al.), perceived in the same way by a child, or are the painful effects equivalent to other traumas at an early age? How do we sort out these influences when a child is burdened with the psychological effects of an acute violent episode and the loss of parents, possibly the culminating event of a history of chronic violence? On the other hand, the psychological effects of chronic violence on a child without these other confounding events might be better isolated if examined in a family characterized by an active factor chronically facilitating violence; research on children growing up with an alcoholic parent was chosen as an example of this type of influence (Rydelius). Finally, the reasons a child himself might become violent can be better understood by examining the components of the intensive treatment provided to a seriously aggressive child and how they supply the nurturance and self-control the family was unable to give (Cohen).

Consistent efforts by diligent and caring parents are too often overwhelmed by the poisonous atmosphere of the neighborhood in which a child lives, a microworld that is the representative of life beyond the family for the child. Our understanding of these noxious influences ought to spawn prevention and treatment activities in the neighborhood (Part III). Surprisingly little is done at this level because of its expense. However, programs utilizing groups already active in the community, perhaps by providing them with additional training, might be not only more cost effective but more humanly effective because of the immediacy and stability of their presence. A program uniting the efforts of clinicians and police in a neighborhood is a model of this type of intervention (Marans).

What is violence from a child's point of view? Does a child distinguish violence as defined by an adult (physical aggression, intense verbal abuse, etc.) from the violent disruptions of nature? Does the child's response to an aggressive earthquake (Moro) differ from his or her response to aggressive actions by adults? Finally, are we even sure what the child's neighborhood is? If the child's neighborhood is moving and changing or is defined according to political vagaries in a distant city, as is the case for refugee children (Malakoff), does this affect them in the same way that violence affects children in a stable neighborhood?

The consideration of cultural influences in Part IV offers the hope that they might be altered favorably for large numbers of children. Political and economic planning presents difficult choices, choices that some regard as instigators of violence when they leave too many families and children with no path to a better life (Celia). Other cultural influences can be more subtle but endowed with the power of laws governing what a nation regards as violence and what aggressive behaviors of citizens are accepted as legitimate in specially defined circumstances. The traditional definition of the right to kill in self-defense in the American West, embedded in controversies of English and American law, shows the powerful influences such decisions can have on the role of violence in the lives and philosophies of its citizens (Brown).

Finally, can a culture identify the influences of emerging technology and recognize that the distinctions among these familial-cultural levels are evaporating? The pervasive influence of television on children, joining influences at family, neighborhood, and national levels, has been obvious but difficult to confront in the United States (Centerwall). Yet we have to ask whether we have unleashed a new technique through which we teach our children violent behavior.

Possibly the most difficult aspect of these reflections on violence in the lives of children is the need to confront the ways in which we cultivate violence in children (Young and Chiland). Nevertheless, the flower arising among these thorns is that such influences can guide us toward strategies to reduce the emergence of so much unnecessary violence in future generations.

I

Violence toward Children, Violence within Children

This section poses questions concerning the psychology and biology of aggression and violence. Is the adult view of aggression clear and understandable for children, in particular in regard to when it is permitted and when not? If not, how are the complexities and peculiarities of our attitudes toward aggression communicated to our children, who are learning from us? We ask because we recognize that contradiction and discordance create confusion and conflict, giving a greater likelihood that individuals will act according to their own rules. This is especially true for children, who are still learning our social rules.

When humans are violently aggressive is it because this quality is inherited? Does it usually indicate some type of brain dysfunction? Are attempts to moderate violence in society naive because our innate biology drives us to violence? What do we know about the brain mechanisms underlying aggression and violence? Is there a brain region or chemical or hormone that controls aggression and violence? Can abnormalities in any such factors be shown to be the bases for violent aggression? Have the brain sciences provided information that will enable psychiatrists to improve diagnostic methods so that violent individuals can be recognized — or that will guide improved treatment, particularly with new medications? Does research help us understand why humans — or animals in general — are aggressive? Are there different types of aggression in humans?

1

Human Violence

COLETTE CHILAND

As child psychiatrists or members of allied professions, we have chosen to dedicate ourselves to the protection of childhood, making use of all that will favor the development of children and attempting to cure the illnesses and handicaps that affect them. We are therefore particularly sensitive to violence against children, though we cannot fail to recognize that children also use violence. Before undertaking the study of violence suffered or committed by children, it is imperative that we reflect on human violence in general, to establish the framework and limits of psychiatric, psychological, and educational activities.

SOME PARADOXES

Yesterday I had some friendly commercial exchanges with my neighbor from the other side of the border. The official languages of our two countries are different, but our *patois*, our vernacular languages, are similar, as are our habits and customs. Today we are starting a war. One of our governments decided to launch an attack and the other one has retaliated by officially declaring war. My neighbor over the border, as an individual, never did any harm to me. What is more, our children played together, and tomorrow one of mine might have married one of his. Here we are, each equipped with a helmet and a gun and pledged to kill one another should we find ourselves face to face. It will be easier for us to anonymously kill the unknown "enemy."

At school, where secular education took the place of religious education, we were taught that to kill our neighbor was forbidden. The law of our country makes homicide a crime, the seriousness of which is increased in cases of premeditation. From one day to the next, everything has been turned upside down; what was previously forbidden to me is now ordered. If I decline, I will be punished as a draft evader or deserter. Invoking my freedom of conscience is not an option—"conscientious objection" will very rarely and with difficulty be recognized, and the substitution of civilian service, distinct from the obligation of bearing arms, will very rarely and with difficulty be allowed. As an individual, I am crushed by the state. Violence is done to me, but I am told it is necessary for public order and for the defense of my country.

Being a doctor, I might have the luck, if I may say so, to serve in the medical corps. My friend in the army has just risked his life in "an engagement of the armed forces." He escaped bullets, shells, and mines. Men have fallen, and our stretcher bearers risk being blown up by mines in order to go pick them up on the battlefield. They pick up all the wounded, our own and those of the "enemy." And now, even though we are tired, we are going to spend hours sewing up, repairing, and saving the life of the enemy, who, fallen to the ground, is again a neighbor, toward whom I have obligations.

We can therefore kill if we kill according to the rules. Violence has both legitimate and illegitimate uses. Who defines legitimacy? Whoever holds the power? Political power proclaims the law. But can we not invoke an unwritten law against the written law, an ethical law above the law of the power at the moment? During the occupation in France, the play *Antigone* by Sophocles took on for us considerable symbolic importance. Antigone wants to bury her brother against the will of her uncle Creon; there is a law above the law of the tyrant. Charles de Gaulle, a career military officer accustomed to obedience, had to have uncommon strength of character to issue his call of 18 June 1940 to organize the struggle for a free France.

Docility and respect for the law, and for the established order, is not enough. We expect a human being to know why he or she submits to one law and rebels against another. But in conflicts between human groups, how do we know and decide which is the *just* cause?

FORCE AND VIOLENCE

Violence can be defined as an abuse of force, though all force is not necessarily violent. Human beings use physical force to survive—to hunt, to find food, to find shelter. In contrast with animals, however, humans exert their force beyond the limits necessary for survival (cf. Lorenz 1963). Wild animals hunt and kill to feed themselves. It is an astonishing spectacle in the jungle to see antelopes peacefully grazing a few feet away from satiated lions and lionesses (it is the lioness who hunts to feed the lion). These animals will not kill just to kill. While they do defend their territory—the male his females, the female her cubs—an attacker in a position of weakness has but to flee or show ritualized signs of submission and is not killed. Only human beings hunt for the pleasure of hunting and destroy animals that do not attack them.

"Defend yourself," says the mother to her young son who complains about his peers. Where does legitimate defense end and gratuitous aggression begin? Cultural beings, humans see as outsiders, and by the same token feel threatened by, those who are "different." The difference can be in appearance, in the color of the skin, in a language we do not understand, in manners, and beliefs. Why are these differences so threatening?

The territory of human beings is not limited to the lair, the house, the country. It is a territory with invisible borders, a world of images in which the human being is more deeply immersed than any other living creature. What makes human beings "superior"— their power of mental representation of the world—is at the same time the source of their particular dangerousness. As much for the individual as for the group, the feeling of being threatened, attacked by all belief that is not one's own, is visceral. To control this initial reflex, to go beyond this defensive intolerance, requires considerable work. The world of ideas is invisible, untouchable, and we confirm its existence through shared convictions. The outsider does more than attack my beliefs—he threatens my world based on the sole fact that he lives in another world. How can there be several truths, several ways? These contradictions are exemplified by religious struggles that become a conflict of powers. In 1685 Louis XIV revoked the Edict of Nantes (1598), which defined the rights of Protestants in France and permitted peace for almost one hundred years. Obviously Louis XIV could not tolerate a state within the state, power other than his own; but above all, freedom of conscience is a threat to the foundation of power — any means is justified to subdue the spirit. The result was the system of dragonnades, soldiers billeted in Protestant houses in the Cévennes region and authorized, in fact urged, to steal property and rape women until a religious conversion followed. Collisions of beliefs and ideas continue in our century, confronted with what is happening in Ireland, in the former Yugoslavia, between Shiite and Sunni Muslims . . . Where is progress? Is it limited to the destructive force of technology?

TERROR

Natural catastrophes leave adults destitute and traumatize children all the more since their parents are unable to support them because they are dead, have disappeared, or are overcome by their own suffering. But violence linked to natural catastrophes, suffered in an often unpredictable manner and against which it is difficult to protect oneself, has not taught humans to avoid making it worse by their own destructiveness. They make war and even define the rules of the game: there are those who respect the laws of war (Geneva Convention) and those who do not respect them. Unconditional pacifism is moreover not an issue: Could we have let Hitler continue his enterprise of death? He came to power *legally*, and *twelve years* were enough for him to discard all rules and establish the reign of hatred (children denounced their parents), systematic extermination, and destruction.

The Enlightenment led the way into the French Revolution and the Declaration of the Rights of Man and Citizen: "Article 1. Men are born and remain free and equal in rights." But the 1789 declaration was followed by the Reign of Terror (1792–1794). In all great revolutions, in all movements of rebellion, there coexist generous ideas and the unleashing of destructive personal passions. Is it necessary to pay such a high price for progress toward greater social justice? How can we pretend to rally around lofty ideas through persecution and terror?

State terrorism, terrorism against the state, the same absurdity of an extreme, blind violence strikes haphazardly or senselessly wants to destroy all hope of reconciliation. The just are not spared; it is not Hitler who is assassinated but Gandhi, a victim of a fanatic, he who preached tolerance, precisely because he preached tolerance. Our insecurity is then unassuageable: just and generous ideas are perhaps a refuge in the face of disarray but not a protection against adversity.

La gégenne, electric torture, has replaced old instruments of torture long ago relegated to dusty museums. Torture does not belong only to the Middle Ages. We argue the right to obtain essential information to save human lives. But the experiments of Milgram, in which no one hesitated to inflict (allegedly) painful electric shocks on the slim pretext of furthering learning, raise intolerable questions about humankind.

Criminals frighten us, the risk of aggression haunts us. We invoke the criminal violence said to be growing, the insecurity in big cities. However, Yves Michaud (1988) writes that crime rates have been going down since the beginning of the nineteenth century, and the homicide rate was three times lower in France during the 1970s than for the period 1830–1852. "In any case, if there is an increase in violence, it is not only on the side of criminality, but rather that we have become extraordinarily sensitive to a level of safety that has never been so low" (pp. 36–37). Why don't Tokyo or Seoul experience the same lack of safety found in New York, São Paulo, or Paris, since they are just as vast and populated? Does it reflect cultural differences, the lack of massive immigration . . . ?

From the study of war to criminology, we barely have the sense of being any closer to the possible control of human violence. As mental health professionals for children, we turn toward the history of individuals in order to attempt to understand what makes them criminals or terrorists. Certain theories (Lombroso) have attempted or are still attempting (the XYY chromosomal karyotype) to link criminality to the biological equipment; even if males are more aggressive than females, testosterone plays a role that is reinforced by education (see Fischer, 1992; Lézine and Stambak, 1959; Maccoby, 1988, 1990; Maccoby and Jacklin, 1974; Money, 1992; Money and Ehrhardt, 1972; Moser, 1987; Tap, 1985). In all cultures, males have to prove themselves. Formerly, it was a demonstration of physical force and courage to kill a lion or to bring back the heads or scalps of warriors. But no biological fate programs certain individuals for aggressivity (see Karli 1982, 1987).

Violence destroys humanity, which can only survive by trying to keep violence in check. René Girard (1972) has proposed the idea of a fundamental violence, the intrinsic violence being deep-rooted within the culture and represented in the sacrifice of a scapegoat (*La violence et le sacré*). In other words, if we attempt to translate the language of Girard through his myth and his rituals, all cultures commemorate their unity founded on a shared and devious hatred. Girard (1978) completes his theory with a nonsacrificial reading of Judeo-Christian Scripture (*Des choses cachées depuis la fondation du monde*), in which social unanimity is established not through hatred of a scapegoat but through the transcendence of love.

All social groups treat other social groups as barbarians. Following the end of World War II, it was believed that only Germans were capable of creating the universe of concentration camps, a methodically organized destruction. But the Gulag, the wars of Algeria, of Vietnam, the reign of Khmer Rouge have taught us that systematic destruction of humans by humans was a potentiality common to all. The question is this: How did we come to such a point, or What can we do to avoid getting there? It is no longer a matter of managing the exceptional, monstrous quality characteristic of some individuals or certain people; it is a matter, according to André Glucksmann (1991), that nothing that is inhuman is foreign to us.

ABUSED CHILDREN, ABUSING PARENTS

A decisive step has been made in our ability to treat abusive parents when we discover that, very often, they also were abused as children. We have been able to overcome the counter-attitude of rejection they provoke in us when we are confronted with the story of the cruelty they inflicted on the child, a story that, often, the parents do not hesitate to elaborate themselves, so much does their attitude seem legitimate to them: they were expecting that the child would be a good parent who loves them and repairs them, the good parent that they never had themselves; the child was only a child who cried, screamed, got herself dirty, needed to be protected, and was not capable of protecting them.

Are there more abused children today than in the past? This theory has been supported by Ariès (1980), without a solid basis.

If we remember the ease with which children were sent to wet nurses and died there like flies, if one remembers the age in which children were sent to work in the fields, in the factories, or in the mines, the life of today's schoolchildren seems a golden one. Why don't they appreciate their luck in being able to go to school? Why are they are so resistant to learning? Reading, writing, mathematics, studying the texts of great thinkers, reflecting instead of being subjected to suffering — isn't that the royal way toward the struggle against violence? Freud, treated as a pessimist when he introduced a mythic opposition between Eros and Thanatos to explain what he observed in the sick individual as well as within the culture, wrote at the end of his letter of 1932 to Einstein, *Why War?*: "But one thing we *can* say: whatever fosters the growth of civilization works at the same time against war." Is Freud, and we tend to think like him, mistaking his wishes for realities? Is this *wishful thinking*?

Our explanation of misdeeds by the adult that takes into account the sufferings inflicted during childhood is part of this cultural work, in which we seek to understand before judging. But there is a limit: we must not take responsibility away from the parents. We cannot avoid confronting them with the serious failure in their task as parents.

Concerning sexual abuse, incest, we have heard of colleagues who are following cases in prison, incestuous fathers or rapists, saying that treatment was possible, but only following confrontation with the reality that a law was transgressed and the imposition of a penalty (Balier, 1988). We hear much more talk these days about incest. Is the incidence of incest increasing, or we are simply more aware? Is incest a result of transient cultural changes or are the prohibitions disappearing? Or is it a result of hearing what children are saying, who formerly did not have the right to speak out? We have noted that most sexual abusers were themselves abused in childhood. To note it, to understand it, is not to excuse it but is an attempt to break the vicious cycle of violence.

VIOLENT CHILDREN

In the same way that we attempt to understand abusing parents through their own histories, we attempt to understand violent children through their own histories. Muriel Gardiner

(1976) has expressed this very eloquently in her book *The Deadly Innocents*. The murderers she talks about are adolescents. Her title for the French edition, *ces enfants voulaient-ils tuer*, means "Did these children want to kill?" It is rare, very rare, that children under 13 years of age are murderers. However, from time to time, such a situation does occur, stirring up much public debate about how they should be punished and why these children murdered.

Violent children who commit crimes or serious offenses have often been submitted to particularly adverse conditions. Their pathology is as much social as it is psychological. Children of the street, of the *favelas,* migrants who are the most deprived of all, of the Fourth World, lack food as much as love. And these last decades have added the problem of drugs. Enticed by dealers, children become sellers themselves to earn their daily dose. The solution involves social measures, and child psychiatrists can only contribute to it.

What remains is the enigma of the invulnerable child. How do certain children resist abuse by rebelling against it and by promising themselves not to succumb to it when they reach adulthood? Most abused children hide their unhappiness from others; they protect their parents from whom they never stop hoping to receive love, they legitimize the abuse they are suffering, and questioned or invited to play psychodrama scenes, they get ready to inflict abuse against their children, who might resist them. But some are successful in splitting away from their parents; favorable encounters with adults or benevolent peers play a decisive role, in spite of the tendency of the abused child to reproduce the experience of abandonment and abuse. It is often only after a long time that the benefit of these positive experiences appears.

The child psychiatrist and the members of his or her team must display immeasurable patience and not limit time spent with the children, especially those who are the most deprived. All brief "programs" leave the children in a state of distress, as again the adult will be missing. This is a vital point that should be understood by all who are in charge of deciding mental health programs. What has been started should not be interrupted.

CONCLUSION: OUR MISSION

It is relatively easy to testify to our good will toward the children who come to see us, brought in by their parents or by a third party, or sometimes on their own. We still have to steel ourselves against their assault on the positive link, against the anguish they make us feel. But we cannot remain closed inside our offices. The child psychiatrist and his or her team everywhere must attempt to contribute to improved opportunities for the most deprived children in existing facilities, such as schools, and to create after-school facilities.

We are all by nature optimists or pessimists about the possibility of "tomorrows that sing." But the meaning of our life is to contribute to the effort of Eros to stand up to Thanatos, as Freud (1930) wrote at the end of "Civilization and Its Discontents."

REFERENCES

Ariès, P. (1980). "From Child King to Child Martyr: Transformation of the Attitude Toward the Child." In *Preventive Child Psychiatry in an Age of Transition*, ed. E. J. Anthony and C. Chiland, pp. xvii–xxi. New York: Wiley.

Balier, C. (1988). *Psychanalyse des comportements violents*. Paris: PUF.

Fischer, G. N. (1992). *La dynamique du social: violence, pouvoir, changement*. Paris: Dunod.

Freud, S. (1930). "Civilization and Its Discontents." *Standard Edition*, 21:59–145.

_____ (1933). "Why war?" *Standard Edition*, 22:197–215.

Gardiner, M. (1976). *The Deadly Innocents*. New York: Basic Books.

Girard, R. (1972). *La violence et le sacré*. Paris: Bernard Grasset.

_____ (1978). *Des choses cachées depuis la fondation du monde*. Paris: Grasset.

Glucksmann, A. (1991). *Le XIe commandement*. Paris: Flammarion.

Karli, P. (1982). *Neurobiologie des comportements d'agression*. Paris: PUF.

_____ (1987). *L'homme agressif*. Paris: Odile Jacob.

Lézine, I., and Stambak M. (1959). "Quelques problèmes d'adaptation du jeune enfant en fonction de son type moteur et du régime éducatif." *Enfance* 1:95–115.

Lorenz K. (1963). *Das Sogennante Böse, Zur Naturgeschichte der Agression*. Verlag Dr. G. Borotha-Schoeler.

Maccoby, E. E. (1988). "Gender as a Social Category." *Developmental Psychology* 24. 6:755–765.

_____ (1990). "Gender and Relationships: A Developmental Account." *American Psychologist* 45, 4:513–520.

Maccoby, E. E., and Jacklin, C. N. (1974). *The Psychology of Sex Differences*. Stanford, Calif.: Stanford University Press.

Michaud, Y. (1988). *La violence*. 2nd ed. Paris: PUF.

Money, J. (1992). "The Concept of Gender Identity Disorder in Childhood and Adolescence after 37 Years." In *Gender Identity and Development in Childhood and Adolescence*. Conference proceedings. London: St. George's Hospital, 3-31.

Money, J., and Ehrhardt, A. A. (1972). *Man & Woman, Boy & Girl*. Baltimore: The Johns Hopkins University Press.

Moser, G. (1987). *L'agression*. Paris: PUF.

Tap, P. (1985). *Masculin et féminin chez l'enfant*. Toulouse: Privat et Edisem.

2

Brain Mechanisms Mediating Aggression and Violence

J . G E R A L D   Y O U N G

J A M E S   R .   B R A S I C

B R I A N   S H E I T M A N

M A D E L E I N E   S T U D N I C K

WHAT IS AGGRESSION?

*The Cultural and Biological Complexity
of Violence*

Violence in the modern world evokes a sense of despair. Centuries of fighting go on unabated, and heinous assaults against innocent victims such as children, for apparently no reason, continue untouched by our moral outrage. Televised documentation of details of this violence strips it of any pretence of glory, courage, or necessity, and individuals are confronted with the reality of cruel bloodshed rather than hearing only of the honorable behavior of soldiers in distant battles won or lost in the past. The routine uncovering of hidden violence, whether massacres initially portrayed as military missions or the physical abuse of children, has altered our perceptions of violence and raised new questions.

On the one hand, neglect of the rise of fascist dictators (through a reluctance to impose a forceful response to their provocations) had disastrous effects on massive populations, while on the other, it is well known that God supports the soldiers of all armies. Similarly, disciplining children is essential to preventing violent behavior as they mature, but abusive parents always have a specific rationale for their behavior. How do we understand the complexity of these behaviors in a way that will help us reduce violence in the modern world? One element that is often a source of confusion is that the underlying biology of aggression is neglected in our hurry to eradicate aggression. Understanding the fundamental biological role of aggressive behaviors for the individual and the species may help us cultivate methods to minimize the unnecessary violence that brings pain to so many.

We will not be able to turn to simple biological concepts to help us: there is not a single brain center, hormone, or chemical substance that controls the brain's activities during aggressive behavior. In fact, multiple brain regions and neurotransmitters (chemical messengers between nerve cells) potentially mediate aggressive behavior, indicating both the complexity of the brain biology underlying aggression and the limitations of our current knowledge. For example, the search for a brain region influencing aggression reveals that aggression in man has been associated with lesions in the hypothalamus, the amygdaloid complex, other portions of the limbic system (Burzaco, 1981), the prefrontal cortex (Bear, 1991), and other parts of the cerebrum (Taylor, 1981). Similarly, various studies of aggression in animals have demonstrated possible influences of a myriad of neurotransmitters and hormones on aggressive behavior, including norepinephrine, epinephrine, dopamine, serotonin, acetylcholine, gamma-aminobutyric acid (GABA), phenylethylamine, beta-endorphin, prolactin, testosterone, other androgens, luteinizing hormone, progesterone, renin, melatonin, and other substances.

Psychopharmacological research with selected drugs might suggest the brain systems predominantly mediating aggressive behaviors. However, the list of classes of medication reported to be useful in the treatment of aggression is similarly remarkable in its diversity, including antipsychotics, mood stabilizers, antihypertensives, antidepressants, sedatives, anxiolytics, anticonvulsants, opiate antagonists, stimulants, antiandrogenic drugs, vitamins, and other classes of medications. In fact, no medication has been specifically approved by the Food and Drug Administration for the treatment of aggression.

The complexity of the brain systems influencing aggression is reflected in the clinical classification of abnormal aggressive behavior. Aggression is so common that no disorder of aggression is recognized. Instead, aggression is a symptom observed in a myriad of neuropsychiatric disorders. Yet, the term *aggression* is mentioned in the criteria for only six disorders in the revised third edition of the *Diagnostic and Statistical Manual of Mental Disorders* (*DSM-III-R*) (American Psychiatric Association, 1987): organic personality syndrome; alcohol intoxication; alcohol idiosyncratic intoxication; sedative, hypnotic, or anxiolytic intoxication; intermittent explosive disorder; and antisocial personality disorder. This poses a dilemma: individuals suffering from schizophrenia, mania, or autism can be aggressive, but no symptom in the definition of the disorders corresponds to aggression.

The agreement from all sectors of research that aggression is a highly complex and multifaceted phenomenon need not discourage us, but suggests that it is a broad construct that requires careful definition and encompasses subtypes that require differentiation. The specific subtypes of aggression would presumably differ somewhat in their neuroanatomical and neurochemical mediation, so that the definition and conceptualization of aggression should accommodate and nurture the opportunities for neurobiological discrimination of subtypes.

Defining Core Concepts Related to Aggression and Violence

The investigation of violence quickly founders on the shoals that wreck so many psychiatric research voyages: definition of the core constructs of complex behaviors is very difficult, spawning ambiguity at the outset and confounding the interpretation of extensive research. The clinician attempting to predict violence when assessing patients recognizes that this is one of the central problems contributing to lower predictive accuracy than desirable (Lidz et al., 1993; Young et al., 1994). The clinical investigator attempting to select a rating scale for aggressive behaviors finds that all have problems that complicate his or her research (Coccaro et al., 1991; Ratey and Gutheil, 1991). Definition of concepts such as aggression and violence is difficult, and relationships among such constructs is the subject of continuing debate. In the *Compact Edition of the Oxford English Dictionary* (Oxford University Press, 1971), the following definitions are provided:

Assertion. . . . **1.** The action of setting free, liberation. . . . **2.** The action of maintaining a cause, or defending it from hostile attack: vindication. . . . **3.** Insistence upon a right or claim. . . . **b.** *Self-assertion*: insistence on a recognition of one's own rights or claims. . . . **4.** The action of declaring or positively stating; declaration, affirmation, averment. . . . **5.** A positive statement; a declaration, averment.

Aggression. . . . **1.** An unprovoked attack; the first attack in a quarrel; an assault, an inroad. . . . **2.** The practice of setting upon anyone; the making of an attack or assault.

Violence. . . . **1.** The exercise of physical force so as to inflict injury on, or cause damage to, person or property; action or conduct characterized by this; treatment or usage tending to cause bodily injury or forcibly interfering with personal freedom. . . . **b.** To inflict harm or injury upon; to outrage or violate. . . . **c.** In weakened sense: Improper treatment or use of a word; wresting or perversion of meaning or application; unauthorized alteration of wording. . . . **d.** Undue constraint applied to some natural process, habit, etc., so as to prevent its free development or exercise. . . . **2.** With *a* and pl. An instance or case of violent, injurious, or severe treatment; a violent act or proceeding. . . . **3.** Force or strength of physical action or natural agents; forcible, powerful, or violent action or emotion (in early use frequently connoting destructive force or capacity). . . . **4.** Great force, severity, or vehemence; intensity of some condition or influence. . . . **b.** Intensity or excess of contrast. . . . **5.** Vehemence of personal feeling or action; great, excessive, or extreme ardour or fervour; also, violent or passionate conduct or language; passion, fury. . . . **6.** Violation of some condition.

In spite of these difficulties, a starting point for any study is required, and one conceptual organization of these related constructs is indicated in figure 2–1. A continuum is hypothesized, in which stimuli potentially eliciting the animal's action toward a goal increase (e.g., obtaining or protecting resources or offspring). This leads to a gradation of behavioral response that can be characterized as increasingly aggressive. The stimuli can be internal or external, and the continuum is considered to involve the sequential elicitation of distinct behaviors. Initially, the animal is not aggressive, but simply asserts itself (e.g., by making its presence known or by a predictable, species-specific signal). This initial stage of assertion is very common, and repeated many times

Figure 2.1 *Relations among Assertion, Aggression, and Violence*

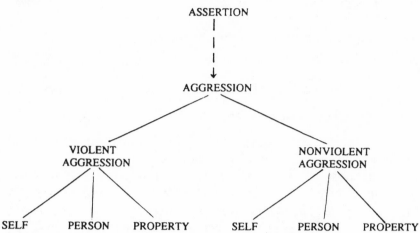

daily by all animals. If the other animal fails to respond to this signal in the manner desired by the first animal, then aggression follows. Nonviolent aggression is conceptualized as leading to neither damage of tissues of either animal nor destruction of any property of the animals. Failure of this verbal or nonverbal signaling stage of aggression leads to violent aggression and damage to property and/or tissues of the combatants. The advantage of this conceptual scheme is that it makes explicit the components of an observable, common sequence of behaviors, so that attempted analysis of eliciting stimuli and modifying influences of each component behavioral pattern might be more fruitful.

The inborn capacities for aggressive behaviors are necessary facilitators of the individual animal's capacity to survive and the species' opportunity to prosper. In spite of ethical and legal restrictions on aggression that are so often at the forefront of our thinking, aggression is sometimes normal and sometimes abnormal or pathological. This is determined by the context of the aggression in relation to expected behavior within the species, and so requires judgments by others of the species. Behavior that becomes too unpredictable within a given context can often lead to aggressive attacks by others. The significance of context also implies that the same behavior can be aggressive in one context but not aggressive in another. Underlying these behaviors are brain mechanisms that have developed to provide both the capacity for aggression and the regulatory capabilities for aggression to be utilized in a maximally adaptive manner. The biological foundation of aggression can be examined at any of several levels of analysis, from observation of a sequence of motor behaviors to dissection of molecular facilitators and inhibitors.

ARE THERE DIFFERENT KINDS OF AGGRESSION?

Ethological Concepts

In order to apply neurobiological methods to the study of mediating brain mechanisms of aggression, units of aggressive behavior must be available for study. The definitional problems mentioned have caused significant problems in the interpretation of these neurobiological studies. However, this problem is common to clinical psychiatric research in general, as in studies of attachment, communication, anxiety, depression, or other clinical phenomena. The boundary discipline between the behavioral and biological sciences is ethology, which is useful in providing conceptual and methodological approaches to the study of behavioral units.

Ethology is an observational, generally nonexperimental science utilizing the comparative study of predictable behaviors of animals within their natural settings, against the background of their phylogenetic origins through mutation and natural selection. Ethology examines these repetitive behaviors by specifying components of each behavioral sequence in a manner that parallels the stimulus–response cycles examined in behavioral psychology or in the information-processing paradigm familiar within cognitive psychology. A behavioral psychologist examines the types and rates of behaviors in relation to contingencies and the training of behaviors, and a cognitive psychologist investigates the mediating processes (sensory encoding, memory retrieval, motor preparation, etc.) between the stimulus and the motor response. In contrast, the ethologist observes the varying stimuli in a natural habitat, identifying those that lead to predictable motor behaviors, and specifying the discrete components of the behaviors. The ethologist generally does not manipulate the features of these sequences in the laboratory, as the natural setting is his or her domain, and ethological methods cast little light on the brain processes intervening between stimulus and response. Nevertheless, ethology makes possible more productive examination of both behavioral contingencies and brain mechanisms underlying behavior.

For an animal, the *appetitive phase of behavior* is that in which he actively seeks sign stimuli because he is driven by an *action-specific energy* that builds up during inactivity of the behavior pattern. This energy is associated with an *innate releasing mechanism,* a sensory mechanism that responds differentially to external stimuli; in the presence of a specific stimulus, the innate releasing mechanism triggers the *fixed motor pattern*, a genetically determined, species-specific stereotyped motor response. This constitutes the *consummatory response,* the phase of behavior through which the action-specific energy is released, consisting of (1) the perception of sign stimuli causing (2) activation of the innate releasing mechanism that (3) elicits performance of the fixed motor pattern. This sequence of appetitive and consummatory behaviors provides the psychiatrist or neurobiologist with specific units to examine in relation to psychological or neural mechanisms, whether appetitive behaviors leading to recognition of signals sought, the sign stimuli themselves, the innate releasing mechanism, or the fixed motor response. Psychoanalysts have been particularly attentive to this sequence, investigating in detail the psychological phenomena associated with aggressive and libidinal drives, which are essentially conceptualized as instincts.

If aggression is a complex phenomenon whose study typically leads to interpretive ambiguity, it is possible that this is because it is not a unitary behavior. It seems reasonable that multiple types of aggression might exist, molded through evolution in response to differing biological needs; specific types of aggression to fulfill these needs would be associated with specific stimuli, because aggressive behaviors are instrumental means for fulfilling these biological needs. Further, if different types of aggression can be identified, it ought to be possible to specify related brain and endocrine substrates for them. In fact, categorizations of aggressive behaviors do exist, although much more experimental validation will be required to determine their utility.

Classifications of Aggressive Behaviors

A first obvious categorization of aggression is based on the *form of the behaviors* in the aggressive animal. The classical contrast is between *affective* and *predatory* aggression (Chi and Flynn, 1971a, b; Masserman, 1941; Reis, 1971, 1974; Wasman and Flynn, 1962). In the *affective* (or "affective defense" or "rage") type of aggression, the animal engages in behaviors such as hissing, spitting, growling, vocalizing, arching its back, retracting its ears, striking and scratching with its claws, and frequent imprecisely aimed biting; pupillary dilatation is evident, and piloerection and sympathetic arousal are marked. Affective aggression commonly occurs when fighting with animals of equal or greater size (usually of the same species) and is less harmful than predatory attack. Affective aggression is subdivided into offensive and defensive behaviors. In contrast, *predatory* (or "stalking" or "quiet biting") aggression consists of locomotor activity such as slinking close to the floor while pursuing the other animal and silent, deadly biting attack directed to the neck and head (typically killing the other animal rapidly) when a prey is sighted; the aggression takes place without vocal or gestural display and little indication of autonomic arousal aside from slight piloerection and pupillary dilatation. Predatory aggression is generally directed toward animals of other species.

Distinct *neuroanatomic loci* are related to these types of aggression, indicating their specificity and apparently distinct biological roles. Affective aggression is associated with stimulation of the medial hypothalamus or the periventricular system (connecting the medial hypothalamus and the midbrain central gray). Increased *offensive* affective aggression follows lesions of the ventromedial nucleus of the hypothalamus; increased shock-elicited fighting consisting of enhanced *defensive* affective aggression results from lesions of the septal nuclei in the rat. Predatory aggression is associated with stimulation of the lateral hypothalamus or the medial forebrain bundle, which connects the hypothalamus with the midbrain tegmentum and the basal olfactory and limbic structures of the forebrain (Chi and Flynn, 1971a, b; Eichelman, 1992; Roberts and Kiess, 1964).

A second basis for classification is the *type of stimulus situation* that elicits the destructive behavior. An example is the classification system suggested by Moyer (1968) that, while not validated by other investigators, has been seminal in fostering attempts to differentiate specific types of aggression that can be shown to have distinct neuroanatomic/physiologic substrates. He established operational definitions of each class of aggression and reviewed research findings suggesting possible neuroanatomic bases for some of them; the status of his classification system when he reviewed existing research is as follows (Moyer, 1968):

Predatory aggression: The presence of a natural object of prey stimulates this class of aggression. Movement by the prey enhances the likelihood of attack, but is not necessary.

Predatory aggression is particularly associated with the function of the lateral hypothalamus. In addition, removal of the amygdala inhibits predatory aggression, while frontal lesions probably facilitate it. Gonadal hormones have little effect.

Intermale aggression. The presence of a male of the same species who is a stranger (i.e., the attacker has not habituated to him) stimulates this type of aggression; specific "submissive" postures by that male inhibit this aggression. It is important to recognize that the attack occurs without provocation by the victim.

The septal area of the brain is probably associated with intermale aggression, but little is known about its neuroanatomical basis. The development of intermale aggression is highly dependent on the presence of the male hormone.

Fear-induced aggression. The stimulus is a sequence of situations. It begins with the presence of an agent threatening to a defensive animal confined in a space that prevents escape. Fear is exhibited, and escape attempts by the defensive animal are necessary to identify this type of aggression in which the cornered animal then turns to attack the attacker.

Lesions in the amygdala and other temporal areas decrease fear-induced aggression, while it is increased by lesions in the septum and ventromedial nucleus of the hypothalamus and by stimulation in the hypothalamus anterior to the ventromedial nucleus. There is little information about any possible endocrine influences.

Irritable aggression. The stimulus for irritable aggression is broad and nonspecific, but it is facilitated by frustration, deprivation, and pain. Any organism (or inanimate object) that can be attacked is sufficient stimulus, and the attack is associated with anger or rage.

The ventromedial hypothalamus is especially associated with irritable aggression, but its role is unclear because irritable aggression is facilitated by either stimulation or removal of this region.

Irritable aggression is decreased by removal of the amygdala and by stimulation of the caudate nucleus and the septum. Castration reduces irritable aggression.

Territorial defense. The stimulus situation consists of an intruder entering a region in which an animal has established itself. The intruder is attacked unless it moves away from the territory. The intruder is usually another animal of the same species, but animals of some species will attack any intruder. The attack will not take place if the defending animal is outside its established territory.

Little is known about the neurobiology of aggression related to territorial defense. There are a few suggestive findings that reproductive hormones influence this class of aggression.

Maternal aggression. The stimulus situation includes a threatening agent coming near to the offspring of the female. As the threatening agent comes nearer to the young, the mother becomes more aggressive.

The neural substrate for this type of aggression has not been identified. Some evidence suggests a role for reproductive hormones.

Instrumental aggression. The expression of aggression by an animal (including any of the previously described types of aggression) can lead to a change in the environment that will reinforce the aggressive behavior of the animal and enhance the likelihood of aggressive behavior in future similar situations. Any of the above stimulus situations can elicit instrumental aggression, which is a learned response.

The brain areas and endocrine factors active in instrumental aggression would include any of the above involved in a specific type of aggression, together with the neural systems underlying all instrumental learning.

Moyer (1968) also postulated the existence of *sex-related aggression*, which consists of aggressive responses to the same stimuli that produce sexual responses. While commonly described in news reports, the lack of clinical or research data at that time suggested that this potential class of aggression be put aside until further information was developed.

These classes of behavior overlap somewhat, and more than one type can be elicited simultaneously by multiple classes of stimuli, but Moyer (1968) described stimulus conditions that differentiate the classes of aggression from one another. While data is insufficient so far, the intuitive sense that different adaptive motivations for aggressive responses might have differing neural and neuroendocrine foundations suggests the utility of continued efforts to discriminate units of appetitive and consummatory aggressive behaviors.

Is there evidence from clinical research with humans that such classes of aggression might exist, and that clinical ethological methods might be employed? Little has been attempted along these lines, but there are distinct possibilities for the future, such as utilizing videotapes (Crowner et al., 1991).

These subtypes of behavior appear to be straightforward, but environmental conditions that frustrate an individual's basic needs are common and continually act as potential provocations to aggression that become difficult to distinguish. In these circumstances alterations in stimuli emitted by individuals, or inaccuracies in the interpretation of stimuli by individuals, might be more frequent and act as additional causes of aggressive behavior. The class designated as irritable aggression is one that can encompass many possible situations eliciting aggression because it reflects nonspecific, common phenomena like frustration. This might be the basis for the increase in many kinds of aggression due to social factors thought to facilitate aggression, such as increasing population density, poverty, noise, and boredom.

A state of expectancy of the animal within an environment constitutes a baseline readiness within an average expectable environment. To the extent that the animal experiences novelty in the environment related to a critical function (e.g., access to resources or a mate) the possibility of aggressive behavior by the animal is increased. The animal is required to make an interpretation of such stimuli, but the encoding of the stimuli by the animal can be altered in a way that facilitates aggression. For example, infectious illness, the stress of floods, or a psychiatric illness might alter the capacity of an individual to use these encoding functions in the usual manner. Stimuli that under ordinary circumstances would be appreciated by the animal as innocuous can be interpreted as dangerous and elicit fear or a defense of territory. Similarly, the stimuli emitted by the animal can be altered by the same phenomena. Atypical communication of signs that are usually stable, predictable traits (e.g., posture, facial expression) can alter communication between animals in a specific context so that the expected behavior of the animal does not occur and aggression is elicited from the other animal. The animal with an altered state has given a communicative sign that is typically inappropriate for that circumstance, nurturing the possibility of an aggressive response in the other animal.

IS VIOLENT OR AGGRESSIVE BEHAVIOR CAUSED BY A BRAIN ABNORMALITY?

Neuroanatomy

The search for a localized center for aggression in the brain has given way to gradual identification of the multiple neural systems involved in these behaviors. Much of the research, however, involves indirect evidence for the role of various anatomical structures, and there are other factors confounding interpretation of findings (especially in humans). This led to the view that caution is essential when discussing brain structures active during aggressive behavior. Nevertheless, certain brain regions contain a higher percentage of these neural systems, and lesions in these regions produce identifiable syndromes that include aggression as a significant symptom. It should be recognized that on the one hand, aggression syndromes resulting from significant lesions in these regions appear to be relatively rare, and the relation of the regions to more common forms of aggression in the general population is the subject of further research; on the other hand, it is possible that such lesions are responsible for a substantial percentage of cases of violent aggression among repeat offenders. These regions and their related aggression syndromes will be discussed first, followed by a description of our current understanding of contributions of specific neurotransmitter-related neural systems distributed across classical anatomical areas of the brain.

The Hypothalamus

The hypothalamus *monitors the internal state* of the individual. It contributes to aggressive behavior insofar as internal state changes induce aggression and initiates the familiar autonomic activities accompanying aggression. *Afferent (sensory) input* comes from the interior of the body (oral cavity, heart, stomach, intestines, blood composition including hormones and osmotic pressure, etc.). *Efferent output* is to the autonomic nervous system, the pituitary gland and its regulation of the neuroendocrine system, and centers in the midbrain and spinal cord that initiate basic stereotyped movements. Control of these functions in the hypothalamus is exerted through the balance achieved by activities of excitatory and inhibitory nuclei. These functions are essential to life and are not modifiable by experience, so the nuclei always respond in the same way to stimuli (Bear, 1991).

Stimulation of the *posterior lateral hypothalamus* in the intact brain reduces the latency for predatory attack in the cat; in a brain in which the cortex is removed, it causes "sham rage," consisting of piloerection, pupillary dilatation, hissing, and extension of the claws (activities preparatory for an attack). By contrast, stimulation of the *ventromedial area of the hypothalamus* in the intact brain prolongs the latency for predatory attack in the cat.

These and related areas of the hypothalamus subserve many other physiological functions as well, so that syndromes (including aggressive behaviors) due to hypothalamic damage are also characterized by symptoms other than aggression. For example, stimulation of the lateral hypothalamus of the rat elicits feeding behaviors (removal causes starvation), while stimulation of the ventromedial area stops them (removal causes obesity) (Bear, 1991). Identification of these concurrent symptoms in patients with severe aggressive disorders can enable tentative identification of hypothalamic lesions underlying the aggressive behavior.

Example of a hypothetical composite aggression syndrome involving the hypothalamus: Rage attacks and violent arguments (including flushing, threats, scratching, hitting, and biting) uncharacteristic for the individual occur. Aggressive intent and anger may be denied by the aggressive individual, who might warn others to retain a safe distance. Remorse or regret might be expressed afterward. Associated symptoms can include obesity, bulimia, hypothyroidism, adrenocortical hypofunction, hypogonadism, amenorrhea, diabetes insipidus, and episodic pyrexia. The aggressive symptoms might be successfully treated by cholinergic antagonists (Bear, 1991).

The Amygdaloid Complex

The amygdala appears to have a primary role in *memory and new learning* (as does another structure in the temporal lobe, the hippocampus), and to participate in the *linkage of sensory experiences with emotional states. Afferent (sensory) input* is from many cortical sensory systems monitoring the external world. This is complex, highly processed sensory information that has converged in unimodal and polymodal association cortices. *Efferent output* is to the hypothalamus, brain stem, thalamus, cortex, hippocampal formation, striatum, and cell groups in the basal forebrain (Amaral, 1987).

The amygdala organizes and modulates autonomic, visceral, emotional, and species-specific behavioral responses to environmental stimuli. For example, activity of specific amygdaloid regions elicits behavioral and autonomic components of species-specific defense responses (Amaral, 1987). It is possible that the amygdaloid complex has an essential role in remembering the emotional significance of sensory stimuli. For example, a region specifically monitoring object recognition in central vision within the visual cortex of the temporal lobe projects broadly to an area of the amygdala that may be a site for conferring a specific emotional color (e.g., fear or anger) to a visual sensory experience with a specific object. The fundamental importance of this function is perhaps more easily understood by describing its absence due to temporal lobe lesions: an absence of fear when sensory stimuli indicate danger, eating junk or garbage, and choosing anyone who appears as a sexual partner (the Kluver-Bucy syndrome, resulting from bilateral removal of the temporal lobes in monkeys). This function does not link sensory experience with an invariant, preset behavioral output. For example, removal of the amygdala in most monkeys leads to a tame, placid monkey, but in submissive monkeys results in unchanged or enhanced aggression. The previously acquired pattern of linking and consequent behavior can be altered; it is not a simple quantitative change (Bear, 1991).

Example of a hypothetical composite aggression syndrome involving the amygdala: Bilateral temporal lobe damage in humans causes loss of aggressive responses and other features of the Kluver-Bucy syndrome, but is uncommon. A common syndrome is the group of disturbances described as temporal lobe epilepsy or partial complex seizures, in which abnormal temporolimbic excitability only rarely leads to aggressive behavior.

Patients with "temporal lobe seizures," however, may have an "interictal behavior syndrome" that encompasses a predictable set of behaviors, including deepening of many emotions. A focus on moral questions is typical, so that the individual is preoccupied with philosophical and religious questions and may write about them extensively. Intense anger follows a minor transgression of the individual's moral principles; this ethical sense protects him against violent actions, but when he does become aggressive it occurs with clear consciousness and may lead to obvious remorse later. Other symptoms that might occur in the interictal behavior syndrome include an absence of a sense of humor, extreme seriousness, repeated fights (commonly over minor matters that are quite important to this individual), elaborate justifications, a pronounced and persistent sense of being treated unjustly, threats to others because of this, a sincere wish to not be harmful to others, irritability, altered sexual preferences, and a committment to many charitable activities (Bear, 1991).

The Prefrontal Cortex

The prefrontal cortex *integrates information essential for planning and judgment*, particularly through its role in the temporal structuring of behavior (using short-term memory, preparatory set, and suppression of internal and external influences), extracting sets of information, and integrating it into new information contributing to executive functions. The information is derived from the interior of the body, the external world, and the salience of stimuli in relation to prior experience (in the context of reward and punishment) (Bear, 1991; Fuster, 1989; Stuss and Benson, 1986).

Afferent (sensory) input is from the diencephalon (with extensive innervation from the mediodorsal nucleus of the thalamus), the mesencephalon, the limbic system, and multiple sensory association areas of the neocortex (including extensive connections with the inferior parietal lobule, which monitors the external world for relevant stimuli). Other connections from the hypothalamus and temporolimbic structures provide further information from internal and external stimuli carrying emotional significance. *Efferent output* from the prefrontal cortex is reciprocal to those structures from which it receives fibers, with the addition of an important efferent output to the basal ganglia (facilitating complex learned movements and speech). Planning of sequential actions and anticipation of the effects of actions on others flow from these capacities of the prefrontal cortex and its connections to related areas (Bear, 1991; Fuster, 1989; Stuss and Benson, 1986).

Example of a hypothetical composite aggression syndrome involving the prefrontal cortex: Prefrontal cortex lesions sometimes cause increased aggression, apparently largely through disinhibition, but often do not. Damage to the orbital frontal cortex may be associated with transient irritability, and these patients can be aggressive after minimal provocation, attending very little to social constraints and possible consequences of the aggressive episode. Lesions of the orbital undersurface are likely to lead to rapid emotional responses to stimuli, with little concern about possible future results of the behavior. Lesions of the dorsal convexity of the frontal lobe cause apathy or indifference, and a loss of long-term planning.

A patient with a lesion of the prefrontal cortex might be rude, give quick, irritable responses, thoughtlessly inflict minor pain, or engage in minor physical aggression. The anger quickly disappears, and the aggressive individual shows little awareness or concern about the feelings of the person that has been hurt. Other indications of impaired social judgment might also be apparent, such as neglect of work, domestic, or caregiving responsibilities; crude manners while eating; lack of a need for privacy concerning personal activities, and so on (Bear, 1991; Fuster, 1989; Stuss and Benson, 1986).

It must be anticipated, of course, that mixed syndromes will result from damage affecting more than one of these brain areas.

Neurochemistry

Attempts to identify neurochemical indices associated with psychiatric disorders or specific behaviors or symptoms have been frustrating because of methodological challenges. However, clinical findings related to impulsivity, suicide, and aggression have been among the most interesting and replicable in biological studies of psychiatric phenomena over the past decades.

Acetylcholine

Acetylcholine enhances predatory aggression and, to a lesser degree, affective aggression. Injection of the hypothalamus with acetylcholine stimulates a predatory biting attack by a cat or rat, while cholinergic blockers prevent a biting attack (Bear, 1991).

Muscarinic cholinergic receptors in the lateral hypothalamus are a logical target for pharmacological treatment.

Serotonin

Both predatory and affective aggression are inhibited by serotonin. Reducing brain serotonergic activity either by (1) restricting the amount of the amino acid precursor of serotonin (tryptophan) in the diet or (2) inhibiting the activity of the principle synthesizing enzyme for serotonin (tryptophan hydroxylase) causes increases in both types of aggression. Other methods for reducing brain serotonin, such as lesioning the serotonergic cells of the raphe nucleus, also produce increased aggression (Eichelman, 1988).

These animal studies have parallel results in human research, in which the effects of serotonergic activity have been among the most replicable findings in biological psychiatry. Lower cerebrospinal fluid (CSF) levels of the principal serotonin metabolite, 5-hydroxyindoleacetic acid (5-HIAA) are correlated with ratings of a higher likelihood of committing suicide using violent means (Asberg et al., 1976a,b) and increased lifelong patterns of aggressive behavior (Brown et al., 1979). Further research has demonstrated that low CSF levels are related to increased impulsive rather than nonimpulsive violent behavior (Linnoila et al., 1983). A subsequent study confirmed the central significance of a link between low CSF 5-HIAA levels and heightened impulsivity, as opposed to an increased aggressive drive. It demonstrated lower CSF 5-HIAA concentrations in impulsive fire setters than in normal volunteers or violent offenders (whose levels were intermediate to the other two groups, as was their history of impulsive behavior) (Virkkunen et al., 1987). Further studies confirmed this negative association between impulsivity and CSF 5-HIAA, even in normal volunteers rated for verbal hostility (Roy and Linnoila, 1988; Linnoila and Virkkunen, 1992).

Examination of patients with orbital frontal lobe lesions and intermittent aggressive behavior has shown some of them to have lower CSF 5-HIAA levels than do patients with damage to other brain regions (van Woerkom et al., 1977). Research using positron emission tomography (PET) has demonstrated reduced metabolic activity, as indicated by deoxyglucose uptake, in the medial prefrontal cortex of impulsive individuals (Goyer et al., 1991).

Additional research has indicated associations of low CSF 5-HIAA concentrations and impulsivity with (1) a subtype of alcoholism including impulsivity and antisocial behavior, (2) a low blood glucose nadir in a glucose tolerance test, and (3) a disturbance of the diurnal activity rhythm. Coupled with impulsive violent behavior and suicide, these findings have been postulated to constitute a "low serotonin syndrome" associated with serotonin dysfunction, in which important clinical features are mediated through dysregulation of serotonergic influences on the suprachiasmatic nucleus (SCN) of the hypothalamus (Linnoila and Virkkunen, 1992). This nucleus acts as an endogenous pacemaker for circadian rhythms and as a regulator of glucose metabolism and receives serotonergic input from the raphe nuclei.

Degradation of serotonin and the catecholamines occurs principally through the activity of the enzyme monoamine oxidase (MAO). Research in many laboratories has produced collective findings suggesting that low activity of MAO might be associated with sensation seeking, impulsiveness, suicide, alcoholism, and criminality (Ellis, 1991), but methodological problems encountered in this research continue to cloud our understanding of these findings.

Clinical investigation that treats aggressive patients with new drugs active at specific subtypes of serotonin receptors should help clarify some of these questions concerning serotonergic function in aggressive individuals.

Norepinephrine

Norepinephrine increases or decreases predatory aggression in various studies, but it markedly enhances affective aggression. Reduction of norepinephrine in the brain stem and the frequency of sham rage attacks are associated in the cat (Reis and Fuxe, 1969). A similar relationship between norepinephrine metabolism and fighting has been reported in the rat (Stolk et al., 1974). More fighting is observed in rats with supersensitive beta-adrenergic receptors (Hegstrand and Eichelman, 1983). Drugs that increase noradrenergic activity in the brain, such as piperoxan, tricyclic antidepressants, and MAO inhibitors, increase aggression in rats, while it is reduced by clonidine or propranolol, which decrease noradrenergic activity (Eichelman, 1988). Stress increases irritability and fighting along with noradrenergic activity. Noradrenergic changes might reflect its participation in arousal processes (it is an index of sympathetic activity) rather than specific influences on aggression, and these distinctions await further research.

Clinical research with humans indicates a direct relation between CSF 3-methoxy-4-hydroxyphenylglycol (MHPG) concentrations and a history of aggressive behavior (Brown et al., 1979). The protocol examining CSF metabolite concentrations in impulsive fire setters found CSF MHPG to be lower in fire setters than normal control volunteers, with levels in violent offenders between those of the other two groups (Virkkunen et al., 1987).

Two medications with direct effects on noradrenergic function have been used clinically in the management of aggressive patients. Drugs that block beta-adrenergic receptors ("beta-blockers") are effective in the management of violent behavior in some patients with schizophrenic disorders or mental retardation. It is possible, however, that their effects reflect actions at subtypes of serotonin receptors. Clonidine, a partial agonist at alpha-adrenergic receptors (reducing noradrenergic activity), can be useful in the management of irritability in some patients, particularly during drug or alcohol withdrawal.

Dopamine

Dopamine facilitates predatory aggression and modestly enhances affective aggression. However, whether this is a relatively direct and discrete effect is questionable, as it is for other neurotransmitters studied. Research has indicated that dopamine activates neural systems involved in pleasure and reward, and the role of dopamine during aggression might reflect its effects on reward systems. A recent hypothesis attempting to encompass the nature of many of the functional effects of dopaminergic activity in the brain suggests that salient stimuli with motivational significance elicit telencephalic dopaminergic activity. This activity generates a state in related neural systems in which there is enhanced preparation to respond to significant environmental stimuli (Blackburn et al., 1992). At the least, it is well known that many antipsychotic drugs act through blocking the D2 dopamine receptor, and they are effective for calming individuals during violent outbursts. However, these drugs have many effects, and this action is certainly not a specific effect on aggressive behaviors.

GABA

Neural systems utilizing the neurotransmitter gamma-amino-butyric acid (GABA) appear to inhibit both predatory and affective aggression. Concentrations of GABA in the brain of aggressive rats are lower than those of less aggressive rats. Increasing GABAeric activity (through inhibition of a degradatory enzyme or direct injection of GABA) leads to a termination of aggression in mice (Eichelman, 1988). However, GABA also has an excitatory action in some brain regions.

The benzodiazepines, classical minor tranquilizers, act at GABA-A receptors to enhance the activity of the GABA system. They generally decrease aggressive behavior in animals and humans. Clinical studies show them to have effective antiaggressive properties in patients with a variety of psychiatric disorders, including their administration in emergency situations to reduce aggression and to sedate agitated patients. It must be remembered, however, that benzodiazepines occasionally cause "paradoxical rage" reactions.

Other Neurotransmitter-Specific Neural Systems

Emphasis on the above neural systems does not indicate that they are the only, or even the major, neurotransmitters contributing to the regulation of aggressive behaviors. In fact, many others may play important roles, such as opioid peptides, excitatory amino acids, phenylethylamine, and cholecystokinin.

Neuroendocrinology

The major hormone examined in relation to aggressive behavior has been testosterone. Testosterone increases aggressive behavior in both sexes in most of the wide range of animal species in which it has been examined, but in interaction with the animal's previous experience. It has both organizational and activational effects on aggressive behaviors. The evidence is inconclusive for primates, however, as it is for humans. While clinical research with humans indicates that adults with high levels of aggressiveness have higher testosterone levels than those with low levels of aggressiveness (especially when rated by others), the meaning is unclear: other investigators have shown that aggressive and competitive encounters can enhance or reduce testosterone levels in relation to success or defeat in competition, confounding the findings of studies of testosterone and aggression (Archer, 1991).

Research has suggested a high prevalence of increased testosterone concentrations in violent sex offenders, but alcohol abuse confounds this association because it alters testosterone levels and is associated with violent behavior (Reiss and Roth, 1993). CSF-free testosterone concentrations do not differ among impulsive and nonimpulsive violent offenders (Roy et al., 1986). Other sex hormones might influence violent behavior, including dehydroepiandrosterone sulfate (DHEAS) and luteinizing hormone (Reiss and Roth, 1993).

Developmental Influences on Aggressive Behavior

The effects of neurotransmitters, or of neuromodulators such as hormones, are variable, according to how complete their effect on aggression is and the age of the animal. One common classification describes the level of influence of these substances:

necessary stimulation for aggressive behaviors
permissive preparation for aggressive behaviors
facilitating for existing aggressive behaviors

A related view classifies the effects of these substances on aggression from a developmental perspective:

organizing: an influence, early in the development of the animal, that is necessary for the formation of the biological structures required for aggressive behaviors
activating: an influence that initiates the aggressive behaviors in the animal

Such influences might also include environmental responses that have significant effects on the development and activation of aggressive behaviors at specific developmental periods (critical periods).

An example of developmental influences is the effect of exposure to abnormal levels of androgenic hormones during the prenatal and perinatal periods, which cause enduring changes in the relationships between steroid hormones and aggressive behavior. For example, injections of testosterone to female mice or rhesus monkeys during pregnancy or at the time of birth leads to more aggressive behavior when the young animals later reach maturity. Similarly, girls inadvertently exposed to inappropriate androgenic hormones during fetal development are characterized by a higher tendency toward aggressive behavior later in life, while boys exposed to antiandrogenic steroids prenatally are less aggressive. The roles of other psychsocial factors in the development of these children has not been clarified, however (Reiss and Roth, 1993). Physical violence peaks in late adolescence (Honjo et al., 1982; Marohn, 1982; Szilárd et al., 1988) or early adulthood (Kay et al., 1988; Tardiff and Sweillam, 1982). Violent teenagers are present in suburban and rural regions as well as in cities (Celis, 1993; Fulginiti, 1992; Rimer, 1993). Aggressive persons usually become less aggressive in middle age (Elliott, 1990).

Electrophysiology

Electrophysiological measures are commonly obtained when evaluating a patient with aggressive behaviors in order to find evidence of brain pathology. Electroencephalograms (EEGs) and event-related (evoked) potentials (ERPs) are very useful because they are sensitive to alterations in brain structure and function. However, this sensitivity carries with it the problem that it is difficult to ascertain the meaning of abnormalities that are detected: the wave forms are typically altered in a nonspecific manner, so that it is common to find an increased frequency of EEG abnormalities in childhood neuropsychiatric disorders without specific, characteristic EEG patterns emerging for the illnesses. In a study of "53 chronically treatment-resistant conduct disordered children in residential treatment in New York State," 83 percent showed abnormalities including slowing, generalized or petit mal paroxysmal activity, and temporal lobe pathology (Turgay et al., 1992a).

The EEG is most frequently utilized to determine whether epilepsy has a possible causal role in the aggressive behaviors of an individual. Yet when EEG abnormalities related to seizures are identified, interpretation of their meaning is difficult. Aggression and epilepsy are both more common in individuals with brain abnormalities, and disentangling the relative weights of causal influences of brain abnormalities and seizures on aggressive behavior is a daunting task. The seizure is nearly always a complex partial seizure (temporal lobe epilepsy, psychomotor seizure), which might subsequently generalize. Examples of this type of research are common. Violence was associated with EEG abnormalities in a group of persons admitted to a hospital for persons with mental retardation (Shah, 1992), yet the increase in aggressiveness in persons with mental retardation may be independent of seizures (Hermann and Seidenberg, 1989). Studies have noted a high frequency of seizures in criminals in prisons (Gunn and Fenton, 1969) and in mental hospitals (Gonzalez Pal et al., 1986), but research indicates that other factors are also operative in these individuals. In addition, these are selected samples and the results cannot be generalized to the population at large. Another study found that although epilepsy was more common in prisoners, the epileptics were not more violent (Whitman et al., 1984). Anticonvulsant medications may cause adverse effects including aggressive behavior (Reynolds, 1983). Children receiving psychoactive medications showed more slowing and paroxysmal phenomena on EEGs than others (Turgay et al., 1992b).

Aggression associated with seizures is classified according to the timing of the aggressive behavior in relation to the seizure: *prodromal aggression* (aggressive behavior during the period prior to the seizure), *ictal aggression* (aggression during the seizure, a rare occurrence), *periictal aggression* (aggression occuring after the seizure, including postictal automatisms, postictal confusional states, and postictal psychotic episodes), and *interictal aggression* (aggression occuring in the periods between seizures, in which the relationship of the aggressive behaviors to the seizure or other potentially causal factors is difficult to sort out). All are relatively rare except interictal aggression, which is itself not a common entity (Fenwick, 1989). Characteristics of patients with aggressive behaviors in association with an interictal disorder related to complex partial seizures are described in the section above describing aggression related to temporal lobe dysfunction. Features that favor the diagnosis of a seizure disorder as a cause of aggressive behavior are indicated in table 2–1.

Distinguishing the contributions of factors other than seizures to a possible interictal syndrome (with aggression as a prominent symptom) continues to be a problem. The presence of brain abnormalities, high doses of anticonvulsant medication, poverty, minimal education, fragmented families, and other potential influential factors cloud any effort to assure that the aggressive behaviors are essentially related to the seizures. Nevertheless, some investigators advance an interictal syndrome as a causal

Table 2.1 *Characteristics of Seizure-Related Aggression*

Behavior before the Aggressive Episode
- behavior is normal prior to the episode
- specific triggers for aggression are not present
- aggressive behavior occurs regardless of circumstances: alone, with other people, comfortable or dangerous circumstances, etc.
- the moment of the episode has no apparent psychological significance for the patient, although it may rarely occur during an argument or state of arousal
- sudden change in behavior, which is usually inappropriate to the circumstances

Onset of Seizure-Related Aggression
- sudden, usually occurring in seconds
- shift from normal behavior to aggressive, violent behavior
- aggressive behavior is inappropriate to the circumstances and occurs anywhere
- seizure onset has characteristic features of a partial complex seizure:
  - sudden termination of ongoing behavior
  - staring begins
  - simple motor automatisms occur
  - confusion is evident

Nature of the Aggressive Episode
- duration of one to three minutes
- includes characteristic features of a partial complex seizure:
  - patient's actions are inappropriate to situation, out of character for the patient, and make no psychological sense
  - confusion is evident
  - objects might be broken randomly
  - aggressive behavior tends to be toward those who are physically close, rather than to people with whom the patient has a relationship
- aggressive behavior reaches a maximum within seconds
- if the aggressive behavior is ictal, it then subsides
- if the aggressive behavior is postictal, it may be more long lasting and more complex
- memory for the aggressive episode is usually absent

Conclusion of the Aggressive Episode
- full consciousness may return immediately or slowly, over minutes
- confusion gradually disappears simultaneously
- the patient is puzzled by what occurred
- the patient behaves appropriately
- guilt, apologies, and self-recrimination are usually not prominent

Adapted from P. Fenwick (1989), "The Nature and Management of Aggression in Epilepsy." *Journal of Neuropsychiatry* 1:418–425, with permission.

factor for the aggressive behavior of some individuals with complex partial seizures. One such hypothesis is the existence of a "neuropsychotic-aggressive syndrome" related to multiple factors that can include epilepsy as an indication of neurological abnormalities (Lewis and Pincus, 1989).

"Kindling" provides a useful conceptual approach to an understanding of aggressive behaviors related to seizures. Kindling occurs when repeated electrical stimulation of a discrete brain area with subictal current gradually reduces the threshold for seizures, which are eventually elicited; this progressive evolution leads to a transition to spontaneity, at which point no external stimulation is required to observe seizures. Subsequent research has demonstrated that serial stimulation of a specific brain area can alter specific behaviors of the animal without reaching a level of stimulation sufficient to elicit seizures. For example, chronic stimulation of specific areas determines whether the animal becomes fearful or aggressive without development of seizures. Such behavior might later be sustained in the absence of stimulation. An animal model for irritable aggressive behavior associated with temporal lobe seizures has been developed (Post et al., 1991; Eichelman, 1988; Engel et al., 1991).

Clinical investigation using ERPs suggests that abnormalities of the P300 component occur in samples of incarcerated criminals and individuals with antisocial disorder (Hare, 1978; Raine and Venables, 1988b; Raine et al., 1990b).

Psychophysiology

Convenient, practical measures reflecting brain regulation of peripheral nervous system function have been sought for many years by clinical investigators. Psychophysiologic indices (e.g., heart rate, blood pressure, peripheral blood flow, galvanic skin response, peripheral temperature) have been studied extensively. While they are often sensitive measures, they are nonspecific and reactive to many influences, making interpretation of results difficult. However, improved methods have begun to provide interesting results. Measures such as heart rate and skin conductance differ in samples of children with conduct disorders, delinquents, and patients with antisocial disorder or a history of criminal activities (Kagan, 1989; Raine and Venables, 1988a; Raine et al., 1990a).

IS AGGRESSIVE BEHAVIOR INHERITED?

Breeding of animals for temperamental characteristics has made the heritability of aggressive tendencies in animals well recognized. Animals differ in levels of aggressive behavior, and selective breeding has produced highly aggressive and nonaggressive strains in short periods of time. These strains have clear differences in neurochemical measures (Eichelman, 1992). Nevertheless, tendencies toward aggression in animals can be modified by environment and experience. Attempts to determine genetic influences on aggressive behaviors in humans have confronted the complexity of gene–environment interactions, but persisting efforts hold promise for the future.

Chromosomal Abnormalities

The major sector of research in humans has been case studies of males with the 47-XYY syndrome who were characterized in early research as more likely to engage in criminal behavior or to have a potential for sexually violent behavior. Later research, however, suggested that any increase in aggressive behavior in individuals with this syndrome would occur only in a very small subgroup and that more research is required. Males with this syndrome do not have any biochemical abnormality that has been defined at present.

"Single Gene" and Polygenic/Multifactorial Disorders

Family studies, adoption studies, and twin studies demonstrate genetic influences on the development of juvenile delinquency and antisocial behavior, but apparent genetic contributions to violent behavior appear to be weak according to available research (Bohman et al., 1982; Cloninger and Gottesmann, 1987; Mednick et al., 1984).

Twin research has produced some support for genetic contributions to aggressive behaviors, with higher concordance rates for aggression in monozygotic twins than for dizygotic twins (Eichelman, 1992; Elliot, 1990; McGuire and Troisi, 1989; Tellegen et al., 1988). However, the usual challenges to twin studies—shared environmental influences and other confounding problems (especially in such complex behavioral phenotypes as aggression) — have made interpretation of such findings difficult.

Familial aggregation research suggests the heritability of aggressive behaviors, but shared family, social, and educational experiences have led to controversies concerning the understanding of study results. The influence of many other potentially contributing factors, such as intelligence levels, socioeconomic factors, and so on adds to the ambiguity confronting investigators in this field. In particular, it can be difficult to sort out the heritability of aggressive behavior in the context of other behaviors associated with psychiatric disorders that are inherited in many of the same families.

A recent familial aggregation study focused on a single Dutch family in which some, but not all, males had a history of hostile, erratic behavior. They reacted to mild stress with outbursts of aggressive behavior, including shouting, cursing, and physically assaulting another person. Some of the men engaged in criminal behavior, such as attempted rape, arson, and exposing themselves in public. Their intelligence was low-normal. Five affected males in the family were found to have a point mutation in the gene for the enzyme monoamine oxidase-A (MAO-A), which degrades monoamines in the body (including serotonin, norepinephrine, epinephrine, and dopamine). There was a pronounced reduction of MAO-A activity in skin fibroblasts obtained from these men. The twelve unaffected males did not have the mutation in MAO-A. Presumably, an excess of these monamines, which function as neurotransmitters, would build up because of the aberrant MAO-A, causing altered transmission of information between nerve cells in the brain that might explain the erratic, aggressive behavior of these men. The gene for MAO-A is located on the X chromosome, so females (with their second copy of the X chromosome) are not affected, but can be carriers of the genetic defect. This mutation is rare, and would explain a partial cause of aggressive behaviors in very few people. In fact, even in these individuals the determinants of aggressive behavior are so complex that these results should be interpreted cautiously, with continued attention to other influences (Brunner et al., 1993).

Another genetic perspective indicates more clearly the manner in which gene–environment interactions occur, and the importance of recognizing how other inherited behaviors or behavioral strategies can be significant determinants of aggressive behaviors.

Animal research indicates that there are heritable alternative strategies for coping with environmental demands. Aggressive animals usually show an active response to aversive (noxious) circumstances, reacting with fight, flight, active avoidance, or sustained activity. Nonaggressive animals, on the other hand, adopt a passive strategy, consisting of immobility and withdrawal. These represent two coping styles, whose success is related to the stability or variability of the environment. The active strategy favors the easy development of routines (intrinsically determined behavior), but animals using an active strategy do not adjust well to minor environmental changes; confronted with a stressor they remove either themselves or the source of the stress. The passive strategy favors reduction of the emotional impact of the stress rather than an active response (extrinsically determined behavior). Active, aggressive animals have well-developed routines that enable them to rapidly execute anticipatory responses, necessary for effective manipulation of events in predictable, stable situations. However, this is maladaptive in unexpected, variable situations. Nonaggressive, passively reacting individuals show flexible responses related to their greater dependence on external stimuli, which is an advantage in variable, unpredictable situations (Benus et al., 1991).

The Panel on the Understanding and Control of Violent Behavior of the National Research Council in the United States (Reiss and Roth, 1993, p. 117) sums up current understanding of possible genetic influences on violent behavior by pointing out that they "would have to involve many genes and substantial environmental variation"; that "genetic processes *alone* cannot explain either short-run fluctuations in violence rates over time or variation in violence rates across countries"; and that "in studies of psychological and social influences on violent behavior, the designs should collect the data on parents and siblings that are needed to control for confounding genetic influences, and greater use should be made of samples of twins, sibling pairs, and adoptees to develop a more precise understanding of the relevant genetic processes."

IS CHRONIC AGGRESSION PART OF A PSYCHIATRIC ILLNESS?

Aggression is a nonspecific symptom, the result of a multitude of possible causes that typically interact with one another to produce aggressive behavior in an individual. Determining "a cause" of aggression in an individual is a frustrating enterprise when a psychiatrist encounters the typical constellation of factors in a patient. Aggressive individuals are usually males who are under the age of 40. "Soft" neurological signs, symptoms related to inattention, and EEG abnormalities are common, as are cognitive impairments. More are left-handed than in control subject samples. These individuals more commonly have histories of adverse perinatal events, trauma, and infections. They usually are raised in families from lower socioeconomic classes, with less education and greater prevalence of unemployment. They often grow up in violent families and have a long history of violence themselves that begins in childhood (Lewis, 1983; Lewis et al., 1987). These complex factors make the attribution of causal status to any other influences difficult to validate. This is one of the principal reasons that aggressive behavior occupies such a minor position in standard psychiatric classification systems in spite of its ubiquity in everyday life.

In addition, these individuals often take prescribed or nonprescribed drugs. It is important to recall that medications can cause or contribute to aggressive behaviors as an adverse side effect. There are case reports of violent behavior in persons using benzodiazepines (Dietch and Jennings, 1988) or a combination of alcohol and marijuana (Yaryura-Tobias, 1981). Alcohol consumption alone has been shown to increase aggressive behavior (Jaffe et al., 1988).

VIOLENCE AND THE CHILD'S DEVELOPING BRAIN AND MIND

Brain regions and neural systems that mediate aggressive behaviors have been identified. However, these structure–function associations are highly complex and not reducible to simple answers. Animal research has provided provisional units of aggressive behavior for neurobiological investigation that may correspond to aspects of human aggressive drives. These units become the basis for further behavioral-biological research: separating out brain activity underlying nonspecific phenomena (such as stress responses) and discriminating the neural systems underlying potential discrete subtypes of aggressive behavior (such as fear-induced vs. maternal aggression). This sector of research should gradually generate improved treatment: better educational and therapeutic methods for helping children alter how they emit or interpret stimuli eliciting aggression, and medications with increasingly specific target neural systems to facilitate these behavioral and psychological therapies.

Assessments of aggressive behavior can become more refined. The rare syndromes in which severe aggressive behavior occurs in the context of other symptoms indicating brain dysfunction will be increasingly recognized, and specific treatments will be provided. Clinical neurochemical measures have begun to have true utility with the repeated validation of the significance of low serotonergic activity. Simple psychophysiological measures might become more informative for identifying subtypes of aggressive behavior and monitoring treatment effects. Improved understanding of aggressive behaviors will foster more practical integration of these symptoms into psychiatric classification systems. Genetic contributions to aggressive behavior will gain clarity through enhanced understanding of mechanisms by which varying temperaments and coping strategies augment or reduce aggression. Rare genetic abnormalities reducing the capacity of individuals to manage aggressive impulses will be identified.

The most significant and optimistic principle emerging, however, is the recognition that genes and neural systems act in anticipation of a continuous interaction with the environment that will mold the brain and behavior. The power of the environment — family, neighborhood, school, culture — to shape nonaggressive behaviors is immense. Other chapters in this volume describe destructive influences on this molding and suggest the path to a future less infected with violence and aggression.

REFERENCES

Amaral, D. G. (1987). "Memory: Anatomical Organization of Candidate Brain Regions." In *Handbook of Physiology*, ed. S. R. Geiger, and V. B. Mountcastle. *Section 1: The Nervous System. Volume V. Higher Functions of the Brain, Part 1,* pp. 211–294.
American Psychiatric Association. (1987). *Diagnostic and Statistical Manual of Mental Disorder.* 3rd ed., revised. Washington, D.C.: American Psychiatric Association.

Archer, J. (1991). "The Influence of Testosterone on Human Aggression." *British Journal of Psychology* 82:1–28.

Åsberg, M., Thorén, P., Träskman, L., Bertilsson, L., and Ringberger, V. (1976a). " 'Serotonin Depression' – A Biochemical Subgroup within the Affective Disorders?" *Science* 191:478–480.

Åsberg, M., Träskman, L., and Thorén, P. (1976b). "5-HIAA in the Cerebrospinal Fluid: A Biochemical Suicide Predictor?" *Archives of General Psychiatry* 33:1193–1197.

Bear, D. (1991). "Neurological Perspectives on Aggressive Behavior." *Journal of Neuropsychiatry* 3:S3–S8.

Benus, R. F., Bohus, B., Koolhaas, J. M., et al. (1991). "Heritable Variation for Aggression as a Reflection of Individual Coping Strategies." *Experientia* 47:1008–1019.

Blackburn, J. R., Pfaus, J. G., and Phillips, A. G. (1992). "Dopamine Functions in Appetitive and Defensive Behaviours." *Progress in Neurobiology* 39:247–279.

Bohman, M., Cloninger, C. R., Sigvardsson, S., et al. (1982). "Predisposition to Petty Criminality in Swedish Adoptees: I. Genetic and Environmental Heterogeneity." *Archives of General Psychiatry* 39:1233–1241.

Brown, G. L., Goodwin, F. K., Ballenger, J. C., et al. (1979). Aggression in Humans Correlates with Cerebrospinal Fluid Amine Metabolites." *Psychiatry Research* 1:131–139.

Brunner, H. G., Nelen, M., Breakefield, X. O., et al., (1993). "Abnormal Behavior Associated with a Point Mutation in the Structural Gene for Monoamine Oxidase A." *Science* 262:578–580.

Burzaco, J. (1981) "The role of some limbic structures in aggressive behavior." In *Biological Psychiatry 1981*, ed. C. Perris, G. Struwe, and B. Jansson. Amsterdam: Elsevier/North-Holland Biomedical Press, 1223–1227.

Celis, W., III. (1993). "Suburban and Rural Schools Learning That Violence Isn't Confined to the Cities." *New York Times*, 21 April, B11.

Chi, C. C., and Flynn, J. P. (1971a). "Neural Pathways Associated with Hypothalamically Elicited Attack Behavior in Cats." *Science* 171:703–706.

_____ (1971b). "Neuroanatomic Projections Related to Biting Attack Elicited from Hypothalamus in Cats." *Brain Research* 35:49–66.

Cloninger, C. R., and Gottesmann, I. I. (1987). "Genetic and Environmental Factors in Antisocial Behavior Disorders." In *The Causes of Crime: New Biological Approaches*, ed. S. A. Mednick, T. E. Moffitt, and S. A. Stack. New York: Cambridge University Press, 92–109.

Coccaro, E. F., Harvey, P. D., Kupsaw-Lawrence, E., et al. (1991). "Development of Neuropharmacologically Based Behavioral Assessments of Impulsive Aggressive Behavior." *Journal of Neuropsychiatry* 3:S44–S51.

Crowner, M. L., Douyon, R., Convit, A., and Volavka, J. (1991). "Videotape Recording of Assaults on a State Hospital Inpatient Ward." *Journal of Neuropsychiatry* 3:S9–S14.

Dietch, J. T., and Jennings, R. K., (1988). "Aggressive Dyscontrol in Patients Treated with Benzodiazepines." *Journal of Clinical Psychiatry* 49(5):184–188.

Eichelman, B. (1988). "Toward a Rational Pharmacotherapy for Aggressive and Violent Behavior." *Hospital and Community Psychiatry* 39:31–39.

———— (1992). "Aggressive Behavior: From Laboratory to Clinic: Quo Vadit?" *Archives of General Psychiatry* 49:488–492.

Elliott, F. A. (1990). "Neurology of Aggression and Episodic Dyscontrol." *Seminars in Neurology* 10:303–312.

Ellis, D. (1991). "Monoamine Oxidase and Criminality: Identifying an Apparent Biological Marker for Antisocial Behavior." *Journal of Research in Crime and Delinquency* 23:227–251.

Engel, J., Jr., Bandler, R., Griffith, N. C., et al. (1991). "Neurobiological Evidence for Epilepsy-Induced Interictal Disturbances." *Advances in Neurology* 55:97–111.

Fenwick, P. (1989). "The Nature and Management of Aggression in Epilepsy." *Journal of Neuropsychiatry* 1:418–425.

Fulginiti, V. A., (1992). "Violence and Children in the United States." *American Journal of Diseases of Children* 146:671–672.

Fuster, J. M. (1989). *The Prefrontal Cortex: Anatomy, Physiology, and Neuropsychology of the Frontal Lobe.* New York: Raven Press.

Gonzalez Pal, S., Delgado Suarez, I. S., Dueñas Becerra, J., et al. (1986). "Violencia y epilepsia." *Revista del Hospital Psiquiatrico de La Habana* 27(3):393–398.

Goyer, P. F., Andreason, P. J., Semple, W. E., et al. (1991). "PET and Personality Disorders." *Biological Psychiatry* 29:94A.

Gunn, J., and Fenton, G., (1969). "Epilepsy in Prisons: A Diagnostic Survey." *British Medical Journal* 4:326–328.

Hare, R. D. (1978). "Electrodermal and Cardiovascular Correlates of Psychopathy." In *Psychopathic Behavior: Approaches to Research,* ed. R. D. Hare and D. Schalling. New York: Wiley.

Hegstrand, L., and Eichelman, B. (1983). "Increased Shock-Induced Fighting with Supersensitive beta-Adrenergic Receptors." *Pharmacology, Biochemistry, and Behavior* 19:313–320.

Hermann, B. P., and Seidenberg, M., eds. (1989). *Childhood Epilepsies: Neuropsychological, Psychosocial and Intervention Aspects.* Chichester: Wiley, 237.

Honjo, S., Sugiyama, T., Wakabayashi, S., et al. (1982). "Family

Violence in Childhood and Adolescence." *Jido Seishai Igaku To Sonokinetsu Ryoiki* 23(2):110–123.

Jaffe, J. H., Babor, T. F., and Fishbein, D. H. (1988). "Alcoholics, Aggression, and Antisocial Personality." *Journal of Studies on Alcohol* 49(3):211–218.

Kagan, J. (1989). "Temperamental Contributions to Social Behavior." *American Psychologist* 44:668–674.

Kay, S. R., Wolkenfeld, F., and Murrill, L. M. (1988). "Profiles of Aggression among Psychiatric Patients: I. Covariates and Predictors." *Journal of Nervous and Mental Disease* 176(9):547–557.

Lewis, D. O. (1983). "Neuropsychiatric Vulnerabilities and Violent Juvenile Delinquency." *Psychiatric Clinics of North America* 6(4):707–714.

Lewis, D. O., and Pincus, J. H. (1989). "Epilepsy and Violence: Evidence for a Neuropsychotic-Aggressive Syndrome." *Journal of Neuropsychiatry* 1:413–418.

Lewis, D. O., Pincus, J. H., Lovely, R., et al. (1987). "Biopsychosocial Characteristics of Matched Samples of Delinquents and Nondelinquents." *Journal of the American Academy of Child and Adolescent Psychiatry* 26(5):744–752.

Lidz, C. W., Mulvey, E. P., and Gardner, W. (1993). "The Accuracy of Predictions of Violence to Others." *Journal of the American Medical Association* 269:1007–1011.

Linnoila, M., and Virkkunen, M. (1992). "Biologic Correlates of Suicidal Risk and Aggressive Behavioral Traits." *Journal of Clinical Psychopharmacology* 12(2, suppl.):19S–20S.

Linnoila, M., Virkkunen, M., Scheinin, M., et al. (1983). "Low Cerebrospinal Fluid 5-Hydroxyindoleacetic Acid Concentration Differentiates Impulsive from Nonimpulsive Violent Behavior." *Life Science* 33:2609–2614.

Linnoila, V. M. I., and Virkkunen, M. (1992). "Aggression, suicidality, and serotonin." *Journal of Clinical Psychiatry* 53(10, suppl.):46–51.

Marohn, R. C. (1982). "Adolescent Violence: Causes and Treatment." *Journal of the American Academy of Child Psychiatry* 21(4):354–360.

Masserman, J. H. (1941). "Is the Hypothalamus a Centre of Emotion?" *Psychosomatic Medicine* 3:1–25.

McGuire, M. T., and Troisi, A. (1989). "Aggression." In *Comprehensive Textbook of Psychiatry,* vol. 1, ed. H. I., Kaplan and B. J. Sadock, 5th ed., Baltimore: Williams & Wilkins, 271–282.

Mednick, S. A., Gabrielli, W. F., and Hutchings, B. (1984). "Genetic Influences in Criminal Convictions: Evidence from an Adoption Cohort." *Science* 224:891–894.

Moyer, K. E. (1968). "Kinds of Aggression and Their Physiological Basis." Originally published in *Communications in Behavior Biologi-*

cal. 2:65–87. Reprinted in *Physiology of Aggression and Implications for Control: An Anthology of Readings*, ed. K. E. Moyer. New York: Raven Press, 1976, 3–25.

Oxford University Press. (1971). *The Compact Edition of the Oxford English Dictionary.* New York: Oxford University Press.

Post, R. M., Weiss, S. R. B., Clark, M., et al. (1991). "Evolving Anatomy and Pharmacology of Kindling." In *Biological Psychiatry*, vol. 2, ed. G. Racagni, N. Brunello, and T. Fukuda. Amsterdam: Elsevier, 210–212.

Raine, A., and Venables, P. H. (1988a). "Skin Conductance Responsivity in Psychopaths to Orienting, Defensive, and Consonant-Vowel Stimuli." *Journal of Psychophysiology* 2:221–225.

_____ (1988b). "Enhanced P3 Evoked Potentials and Longer P3 Recovery Times in Psychopaths." *Psychophysiology* 25:30–38.

Raine, A., Venables, P. H., and Williams, M. (1990a). "Relationships between CNS and ANS Measures of Arousal at Age 15 and Criminality at Age 24." *Archives of General Psychiatry* 47:1003–1007.

_____ (1990b). "Relationships between N1, P300 and CNV Recorded at Age 15 and Criminal Behavior at Age 24." *Psychophysiology* 27:567–575.

Ratey, J. J., and Gutheil, C. M. (1991). "The Measurement of Aggressive Behavior: Reflections on the Use of the Overt Aggression Scale and the Modified Overt Aggression Scale." *Journal of Neuropsychiatry* 3:S57–S60.

Reis, D. (1971). "Brain Monoamines in Aggression and Sleep." *Clinical Neurosurgery.* 18:471–502.

_____ (1974). "Central Neurotransmitters in Aggression." *Research Publications of the Association for Research in Nervous and Mental Diseases* 52:119–148.

Reis, D. J., and Fuxe, K. (1969). "Brain Norepinephrine: Evidence That Neuronal Release Is Essential for Sham Rage Behavior Following Brainstem Transection in Cat." *Proceedings of the National Academy of Sciences* 64:108–112.

Reiss, A. J., Jr., and Roth, J. A., eds. (1993). *Understanding and Preventing Violence.* Washington, D.C.: National Academy Press.

Reynolds, E. H. (1983). "Mental Effects of Antiepileptic Medication: A Review." *Epilepsia* 24(suppl. 2):S85–S95.

Rimer, S. (1993). "No Gang Tied to Killing, Just Three Rare Friends." *New York Times*, 21 April, B11.

Roberts, W. W., and Kiess, H. G. (1964). "Motivational Properties of Hypothalamic Aggression in Cats." Originally published in *Journal of Comparative Physiology and Psychology.* 58:187–193. Reprinted in *Physiology of Aggression and Implications for Control: An Anthology of Readings*, ed. K. E. Moyer. New York: Raven Press, 1976, 31–37.

Roy, A., and Linnoila, M. (1988). "Suicidal Behavior, Impulsivity and Serotonin." *Acta Psychiatrica Scandinavica* 78:529–535.

Roy, A., Virkkunen, M., Guthrie, S., et al. (1986). "Monoamines, Glucose Metabolism, Suicidal and Aggressive Behaviors." *Psychopharmacology Bulletin* 22(3):661–665.

Shah, A. K. (1992). "Violence, Death, and Associated Factors on a Mental Handicap Ward." *Journal of Intellectual Disability Research* 36:229–239.

Stolk, J. M., Conner, R. L., Levine, S., et al. (1974). "Brain Norepinephrine Metabolism and Shock-Induced Fighting Behavior in Rats: Differential Effects of Shock and Fighting on the Neurochemical Response to a Common Footshock Stimulus." *Journal of Pharmacology and Experimental Therapeutics* 190(2):193–209.

Stuss, D. T., and Benson, D. F. (1986). *The Frontal Lobes.* New York: Raven Press.

Szilárd, V. J., Vetró, Á, and Farkasinszky, T. (1988). "Elektive aggressive Verhaltensstörungen." *Praxis Der Kinderpsychologie Und Kinderpsychiatrie* 37:121–124.

Tardiff, K., and Sweillam, A. (1982). "Assaultive Behavior among Chronic Patients." *American Journal of Psychiatry* 139:212–215.

Taylor, P. (1981). "Cerebral Disorder in Violence and Psychosis." In *Biological Psychiatry 1981*, ed. C. Perris, G. Struwe, and B. Jansson. Amsterdam: Elsevier/North-Holland Biomedical Press, 532–535.

Tellegen, A., Lykken, D. T., Bouchard, T. J., Jr., et al. (1988). "Personality Similarity in Twins Reared Apart and Together." *Journal of Personality and Social Psychology* 54:1031–1039.

Turgay, A., Gordon, E., and Vigdor, M. (1992a). "EEG and Dynamic Brain Mapping in Children with Chronic, Treatment-Resistant Conduct Disorders [abstract]." *Neuropsychobiology* 25:74.

_____ (1992b). "Psychoactive Drug Use and Dynamic Brain Mapping (DBM) in Children with Chronic Psychiatric Disorders [abstract]." *Neuropsychobiology* 25:74.

Van Woerkom, T. C. A. M., Teelken, A. W., and Minderhoud, J. M. (1977). "Difference in Neurotransmitter Metabolism in Frontotemporal-Lobe Contusion and Diffuse Cerebral Contusion." *Lancet* 1:812–813.

Virkkunen, M., Nuutila, A., Goodwin, F. K., et al. (1987). "Cerebrospinal Fluid Monoamine Metabolite Levels in Male Arsonists." *Archives of General Psychiatry* 44:241–247.

Wasman, M., and Flynn, J. P. (1962). "Directed Attack Elicited from the Hypothalamus." *Archives of Neurology* (Chicago) 6:220–227.

Whitman, S., Coleman, T. E., Patmon, C., et al. (1984). "Epilepsy in Prison: Elevated Prevalence and No Relationship to Violence." *Neurology* 34:775–782.

Yaryura-Tobias, J. A. (1981). "Alcoholism, Marijuana, and Violent

Behavior." In *Biological Psychiatry 1981*, ed. C. Perris, G. Struwe, and B. Jansson. New York: Elsevier/North-Holland Biomedical Press, 933–935.

Young, J. G., Kaplan, D., Pascualvaca, D., et al. (1994). "Psychiatric Examination of the Infant, Child, and Adolescent." In *Comprehensive Textbook of Psychiatry,* ed. H. I. Kaplan and B. J. Sadock. 6th ed. Baltimore: Williams & Wilkins.

II

Violence in the Child's Family and Home

When violence occurs in the child's home, is there a predictable set of responses in the child, or do children show individual differences? Do children become symptomatic, or is their response limited to short- or moderate-term emotions and moods congruent with the event? Do parents and other adults respond in predictable or diverse ways? Most important, how does violence in a child's family influence his or her development? Does the child become chronically symptomatic later? Is it a predictable set of chronic symptoms, or does it differ according to the violent incident, the family involved, and the individual child? Do we have any information indicating whether destructive behavior patterns leading to violence in families across generations are passed on through genes or through "social inheritance"?

We can demonstrate many factors that distort the development of children in a way that makes them more likely to be violent later, but the multiple contributing factors make it difficult to determine which are most important. Can we make a better judgment about what traumatic factors were most disturbing and destructive to the child's development by examining those components that are essential in the later treatment of aggressive children? Are there basic components in the treatment of aggressive children that make it obvious that these factors were missing or disturbed during the period in which they were growing up?

3

Children Who Survive after One Parent
Has Killed the Other: A Research Study*

TONY KAPLAN

JEAN HARRIS HENDRIKS

DORA BLACK

BOB BLIZZARD

INTRODUCTION

When we began to work with children whose father had killed their mother, we looked for guidance in the scientific literature. At that time (1986) we found only three references (Malmquist, 1986; Pruett, 1979; Schetky, 1978). Since then we have drawn on a substantial and growing body of work on children and violence. In the 1960s the physical abuse of children became an important issue. The next decade led to comparable research on violence to women within the home, but only in the past ten years has there been a coherent debate on the witnessing of violence by children. Children who live in violent families learn that violence is an acceptable way of resolving conflicts. Children of either sex may take the side of the aggressor, blaming their mother, who is usually the victim, for not doing what their father wished, while simultaneously girls learn to accept that being a victim cannot be escaped. These children live with anxiety and

---

*This chapter draws on work published in *When Father Kills Mother: Guiding Children through Trauma and Grief* by Jean Harris Hendriks, Dora Black, and Tony Kaplan, published by Routledge, London, in September 1993, and reprinted with permission.

Our gratitude is extended to Amanda King and Catherine White for research assistance.

uncertainty and are at risk of developing psychosomatic symptoms, problems of conduct and emotions, and of learning unconstructive and repetitive ways of resolving arguments and problems (Rosenberg and Rossmann, 1990). Gelles (1990) offers a critique and overview of current work.

Until as recently as 1985, psychiatrists were skeptical about the concept of post-traumatic stress disorder in children, although this became a diagnostic category in the third edition of the *Diagnostic and Statistical Manual of the American Psychiatric Association* (1980). Garmezy and Rutter, in a standard British text (1985) stated, with regard to the effects of severe stress upon children, "behavioural disturbances appear to be less intense than might have been anticipated; a majority of children show a moderate amount of fear and anxiety but this subsides; aggressive behaviour marked by the clinging to parents and heightened dependency on adults appears and a moderately mild sleep disturbance persists for many months" (p. 162). At that time, studies of disaster rarely dealt with direct effects on children, relying on observations by parents and other adults. A recent body of research, reviewed by Terr (1991), is crucially different in that it relates to direct interviews with and observation of children and adolescents. Work ranges from that of Terr (1979, 1983), which broke new ground and at the time was much criticized by the psychiatric establishment, in exploring the effects of trauma after kidnapping of children on a school bus; to that of Pynoos and Eth (1984, 1986) on children who had witnessed acts of violence, including homicide; to that on children involved in larger disasters. Parry Jones and his colleagues (1992) worked with children who were in the town of Lockerbie in December 1988 when a Pan Am jet fell on their town. Yule and Williams (1990) and Yule and Udwin (1991) studied survivors of life-threatening disasters at sea. Recent distinguished and continuing research is all too readily available from child survivors and victims of terrorism and war (e.g, Ayalon, 1983; Dyregov and Raundalen, 1992; Hermann, 1992). The interacting effects of trauma and grief are discussed by Raphael (1982, 1992).

Often only the children are there when their mother dies, and afterward they may be the only source of information, not just about the killing, but about family life before it. This information may be needed for civil court decisions and by social workers and relatives who try to plan for the children and may be relevant to a criminal trial. At this point it is difficult to exaggerate the plight of the children. They may be too young or too shocked to tell of what they have seen, heard, smelled, or what they feel. The killing may have come out of a clear sky or may have been preceded by other experiences of traumatic violence, by marital quarreling, or by the onset of psychiatric illness in either parent. The children may have witnessed the killing and been left with the corpse. Usually, however, the killer is readily identified and arrested or, on rarer occasions, is dead by his own hand. A majority (90 percent) are killings of a woman by a man; in the minority situation the common scenario is that the killing by the mother is a response to chronic violence from her partner.

The children are dislocated and, unless the crime remains briefly undetected, rarely sleep in their own home on the night after the killing. The initial trauma may be followed by repeated further upsets when they are moved from one temporary foster home to another or placed with relatives, themselves grieving and bitterly angry about the death of a loved one, or shocked and horrified at their relative's part in the death. Commonly, the children become involved in battles between maternal and paternal families that mirror those between their parents, and disputes may also evolve over current finances, possessions, inheritance, and compensation claims. Unless the law intervenes, the children remain in the legal guardianship of the parent who committed the crime; often this parent attempts to continue to control their lives from prison. There is pressing need for legal representation and advocacy for the children. The civil court decisions concerning their welfare must take precedence over and not await the outcome of criminal proceedings that may not take place for many months after the homicide.

SUBJECTS AND METHODS

Since beginning our project in 1986, we have personally seen 111 children from 53 families in which one parent killed the other. We have offered consultation to professionals dealing with children, families, and other caregivers in 9 other cases involving 19 children. Overall, therefore, we have heard the stories of and turned our minds to the difficulties for 130 children from 62 families devastated by the loss of their parents in this cruel way. In

6 cases the mother killed the father; in the rest (56 cases) it was the father who was the assailant, the mother the victim.

The research described in this chapter is an attempt to quantify the information on the circumstances of these children and the impressions we gained from our clinical interviews. We have not used standardized tests or measures; we do not have a control group with which to compare the children we have seen. The group of children is clearly heterogeneous, referred for different reasons (from crisis intervention, through assessment and treatment, to advice on where the child should live and what sort of contact there should be with the surviving parent). They were seen hours, days, or years after their parent's death and with variable regularity thereafter. The children differ in age (see table 3-1). Each child and each family is unique in their history and circumstances, and in the particular set of relationships that shape their family, yet the data do tell a story; patterns begin to become discernible. The study continues.

For technical reasons we analyzed by computer the data on 95 of the 111 children personally interviewed. This represents the findings from forty-five of the fifty-three families seen. In some cases, the data set is incomplete.

The data were drawn from a questionnaire we devised and completed after assessment interviews by whichever one of us was most involved in the case. Uniformity of terms and definitions was agreed at regular joint meetings.

Statistical analysis was carried out using SPSS/PC+ (Norusis, 1990). Group comparisons involving categorical outcome measures were made using the chi-square test and logistic regression. Comparisons involving continuous measures of outcome were made using analysis of variance and multiple regression.

Table 3.1 *Age at Time of Mother's Death*

Age in Years at Time of Killing	N	%
<5	38	40
6–11	39	41
>12	19	18

RESULTS

Characteristics of the Children and Families

Sex and Age of the Children

The group analyzed consisted of 54 boys and 41 girls. Thirty-eight children (40 percent) were aged 5 or under, about the same number were between 6 and 11, and close to 20 percent (19 children) were in their teens when one of their parents died at the hands of the other (see table 3-1). Out of the 45 families, 28 had a child under the age of 5 in it at the time of the killing. This is in keeping with the finding that marital satisfaction is at its lowest when there is a child of under 5 in the household, which probably is reciprocally related to the well-known finding that the more children under 5 there are in the family, the greater the risk of clinical depression in the mother (Brown and Harris, 1978). A further hypothesis is that as a group, the parents were fairly young, or at least early in their marriages when the killing took place. The age of the children when referred to us is presented in table 3-2.

Parental Authority/Responsibility for the Children

For a third of the children, their surviving parent still had parental authority (13 percent) or shared this authority with the local social services (21 percent) at the time of referral to us. In two-thirds of cases, the right to make decisions on behalf of the child had been withdrawn from the surviving parent and was vested in the high court (60 percent) or in the local social services (69 percent).

Ethnicity and Religion of the Parents

In one out of ten cases the parents differed from each other in their ethnic origins, and in one out of twenty there were differences in religion between the parents. Sixteen percent of fathers and 16 percent of mothers were Asian. Eighteen percent of fathers and 11 percent of mothers were from other ethnic minorities. This compares with figures of 2.4 percent Asians and 2.3 percent other ethnic minorities in the general population (Haskey, 1991). In other words, Asians and other ethnic groups were overrepresented sixfold in our sample. With regard to religion, 20 percent of

Table 3.2 *Age at Referral*

Age in Years at Time of Referral	N
1	1
3	5
4	7
5	10
6	6
7	8
8	11
9	3
10	7
11	5
12	5
13	3
14	4
15	4
16	1
18	2
19	2

fathers and 15 percent of mothers were Muslim. In the general population 4.5 percent are Muslim (Muslim Cultural Society, personal communication). Thus, as a proportion there were four times as many Muslim families referred to us as would be expected. In half the families headed by an Asian Muslim man, the parents were first cousins.

Family Structure

In one in four families, the parents had been separated for more than a month at the time of the killing. A smaller number (16 percent) had separated but for a shorter time. Where the parents had separated, the estranged parent (usually the father) managed to maintain regular contact in half the cases; in a quarter, contact was irregular or nonexistent, and for the other quarter we were not able to ascertain whether there had been contact or not. Perhaps surprisingly, 60 percent of families were intact at the time of the killing. This is, however, in keeping with the observation that relatively few women in violent relationships leave their partners (Walker, 1979).

Family Conflict and Violence

There was long-standing conflict between the parents in two-thirds of the families, with the children likely to have witnessed violence between the parents in nearly half the cases. This is almost certainly an underestimate: in a quarter of the cases we did not know whether the children had previously seen one parent being violent to the other. We established that only in thirteen cases was there any evidence of physical abuse of the child. This finding is at variance with findings from research on battered wives that did not end in homicide (for example Jaffe et al., 1990), which shows a considerable overlap between the husband's violence to his wife and his violence to his children or at least to one of the children. It is not clear to us at this stage whether this has heuristic value, which should generate new hypotheses. It may indeed imply that contrary to our expectations, the children we have seen have less in common with the children of mothers who are beaten but not killed. Perhaps, however, it is an artifact produced by seeking the information from the child and in the context of one parent having killed the other. Out of shame or because they blame themselves, children will often hide the fact that they have been beaten by a parent.

Alliances

Only one in ten of the children were closer to the father than the mother before the killing. Given that most children were quite young at the time of the death, this is perhaps not surprising; younger children tend to be closer to their mother. Indeed, half were closer to their mother; some (7 percent) had been close to both. In 30 percent we could not establish clearly what the child's relationship with the parents had been like.

Of the ninety-five children, forty had maternal grandparents closely involved with the family even before the homicide. Twenty-five felt close to both sets of grandparents, ten felt close to neither, and only for five children were the paternal grandparents those they felt closer to. This had implications for placement of the children after the loss of their parents and with regard to their vulnerability to further stresses. (A close confiding relationship with at least one adult outside of the immediate family—usually a grandparent—has been found to protect children against the stress of marital discord, separation and divorce [Jenkins and Smith, 1991].)

Factors Associated with the Homicide

As in other similar studies, sexual jealousy, whether based on actual or imagined infidelity, was the motivation most commonly associated with the homicide (36 percent). Other cited and sometimes overlapping factors include escalation of chronic violence (32 percent), the partner's threat to leave (23 percent), and alcohol abuse (20 percent). Definite evidence of formal mental illness, as indicated by the sentence at their trial, was a factor in 14 percent only (six cases).

Whereabouts of Surviving Parent

At the time of our assessment, thirteen of the surviving parents were still on remand, ten were serving sentences for murder and eleven for manslaughter, nine had served time for manslaughter but had already been released, one had committed suicide, and one was detained in a psychiatric hospital. The verdict of manslaughter was twice as common as that of murder.

Witnessing of the Killing

Twenty-four of the ninety-five children actually saw their parent being killed; a further nine heard but did not see the final violence. Forty-six children (nearly half of all the children) either were not present at, were asleep during, or did not acknowledge their awareness of the killing. In the case of eight children, whether the child had witnessed the killing could not be established.

Immediate Therapeutic Interventions for the Child

Crisis Interventions

Within weeks of the killing, only one in five children had been offered a crisis intervention, which according to our definition meant a critical incident debriefing. In most cases we relied on others to say whether and to what extent this had occurred. In the three cases in which we did the debriefing ourselves, none went on to develop post-traumatic stress disorder (PTSD) in spite of witnessing the full horror of their mother's death. However, this effect of crisis intervention in preventing PTSD could not be demonstrated statistically with the figures available for the sample as a whole. Even when entered into a regression equation with age of the child at the time of the killing and whether the child witnessed the killing, crisis intervention was not a significant influence on whether PTSD was present at the time of the assessment. Perhaps the crisis interventions made were not sufficiently skilled or intensive. Perhaps in part this lack of a statistical association could be attributed to the relatively small number of children offered a crisis intervention and the variable time to assessment after the killing, which was not taken into account in a controlled way. More of the 40 percent seen later than a year after the killing had not had a crisis intervention and did not have symptoms of post-traumatic stress compared with those seen earlier. This will require further statistical analysis. In fact, the only proper way to evaluate the protective and/or ameliorative effect of crisis intervention debriefing is in a controlled prospective study. So far no satisfactory study has been done. The methodological and other issues involved in trying to demonstrate the efficacy of this treatment are reviewed by McFarlane (1989).

What and Whether the Child was Told

We were not always clear what the child had been told about the killing and by whom. Twenty-nine were presumed by their caregivers to know what had happened; thirty-six were told within a week (usually by a social worker), nine were told later (often by a member of a child psychiatry team), and thirteen had still not been told that their father had killed their mother at the time of our assessment. Only very rarely was the child given this information by a relative.

Opportunities For Mourning

Our inquiries revealed that for nearly half of the children discussion or questions about the death of their mother at their father's hands were explicitly or implicitly forbidden or at least discouraged by surrogate parents. One in three had neither participated in any of the funeral rites nor visited the grave of the deceased parent. Only for one in ten was mourning recognized and actively supported.

Relationships and Living Arrangements after the Parent's Death

Conflicts between Kin

In a third of cases the two sides of the families, maternal and paternal kin, were actively hostile to each other. In fact, this probably represents the majority of the families in which there was contact between the maternal and the paternal kin. In only very few of the families where contact continued had they come to terms with the events in a way that did not expose the children to what was tantamount to a continuation of the marital conflict by proxy. In one case this was achieved by the maternal grandparents coming to the father's defense and agreeing that their daughter's behavior had been extremely provocative even as a teenager while living at home.

Placements of the Child

More than half the children went to live with relatives straight after the killing, 35 percent to someone from the deceased mother's family (usually the maternal grandparents), 17 percent to the father's family (again usually the grandparents). About a third went to foster parents, the occasional child went to a friend of the family or a neighbor, and ten children from three families were found places in children's homes (see table 3-3). (The more children there are in any one family, the more difficult it becomes to place them all together other than in a children's home.) At least three-quarters moved on from their first placement within the first year. Most of these moves were planned in the children's interests, although in one in six cases the children were moved because the placement broke down. Some of the most severely affected and

Table 3.3 *Where Child(dren) Went to Live Immediately After Mother's Death*

Immediate Placement	N	%
Maternal relative	33	35
Paternal relative	16	17
Friend	8	9
Foster parent	26	28
Children's home	10	11

hence the more difficult to look after children ended up in children's homes. It is not clear from the data whether it is cause or effect that determines the greater difficulties of those who ended up in children's homes, especially when compared with those that were living with the mother's family (significantly different at the 0.04 level of probability).

At the time of our assessment, at varying lengths of time after the death, 40 percent of the children were staying with kin, 26 percent with the mother's family, and 14 percent with the father's. Almost 40 percent were with foster parents and 20 percent were in children's homes, other placements being unavailable or having broken down (see table 3–4). For most children, where they were living at the time of the assessment was the place that had been home to them for the longest time since their parent's death. Just over 40 percent had had the one placement only; about the same number had two moves to deal with (in most of these cases to an emergency placement and to a planned placement). However, when analyzing these figures it is important to bear in mind that the assessment took place at various times after the killing. That children seen relatively soon after the killing had just one placement or perhaps two is not remarkable; but it does introduce a bias that makes the early picture too optimistic. Nevertheless, thirteen children had already had three or more moves of home, which in itself is high, but especially so for children who were already traumatized and vulnerable and needing stability more than most.

Contact With the Surviving Parent

Only half the children had seen the surviving parent by the time of our first meeting. Again, the timing of the first assessment in

Table 3.4 *Where Child Was Living at Time of Our Assessment*

Placement at Time of Assessment	N	%
Maternal relative	24	26
Paternal relative	13	14
Foster parent	34	37
Children's home	18	20

relation to the killing needs to be borne in mind. Nearly half did not wish to see the surviving parent, and for only a third was contact regular. One in five children had seen their remaining parent, usually the father, in prison but had discontinued this. Children were most likely to have seen their surviving parent in prison if they were living with foster parents; this was least likely if they were living with maternal kin ($p = 0.02$). Children with PTSD were less likely to be in regular contact with the surviving parent ($p = 0.04$). This may reflect their abhorrence or fear of the parent since children who witnessed the killing were much more likely to develop PTSD (see later), or it may be an artifact since the children with PTSD were more likely to have been seen within a year of the killing before regular contact could be established. Certainly a child's having been exposed to chronic violence between the parents did not lead to his or her seeing the incarcerated parent less. If anything, statistically the opposite was true ($p = 0.05$), leading to the speculation that children who witness violence between their parents adapt over time by taking on the parental role, taking care of their parents' needs even to the exclusion of their own. Seeing their surviving parent more often than children not exposed to chronic violence, if indeed this is the case, may be a reflection of a learned compulsion to protect and care for the parent(s).

Psychiatric Symptoms and General Adaptation

Psychiatric Sequelae for the Child

Quantifying the mental health costs of these events for the indirect victims, the children, is complex. It depends not only on the direct effect of the traumas and losses but also on preexisting vulnerability or psychopathology (about which we had very little information in most cases) and on the effects of their current circumstances and relationships on their ways of coping. To simplify the analysis, we used problem or symptom categories rather than isolated symptoms or formal psychiatric diagnosis. Because some problems tend to occur early (e.g., symptoms of post-traumatic stress disorder) and some later (e.g., identity problems), the timing of the assessment influences the rate of recorded symptoms. Symptoms that occur early and then recede and symptoms that only emerge later on will be underestimated.

Table 3.5 *Children with PTSD*

Children Showing PTSD	N	%
Severe	5	5
Moderate	19	21
Mild	20	22
None	41	45

Because there was no suitable control group, the comparisons between different affected groups lend themselves better to inferences than to conclusions. Except for the relationship between crisis intervention and PTSD, we are not able to measure the effects of our other interventions; to do so would require a "no treatment" comparison group, something that seems to us clearly unethical. The analysis we can do relies on "naturally occurring experiments" only. The results convey only impressions, glimpses of the overall picture. A clearer picture may emerge from more formal research at a later stage of our investigations.

Post-Traumatic Stress Disorder

So far we have found that one quarter of the children showed moderate or severe symptoms of PTSD, and another quarter had mild or few symptoms only, often with traumatic nightmares as a single symptom (especially in younger children). Just under one-half had no residual symptoms of PTSD or had no PTSD at all (see table 3–5). Children who had witnessed the killing were much more likely to develop PTSD (p = 0.001) (table 3–6); the child's age, sex, and whether they had a crisis intervention did not add to the prediction.

Table 3.6 *The Relationship between the Child Witnessing the Killing and the Development of Post-Traumatic Stress Symptoms*

	PTSD	No PTSD
Witnessed killing	23	7
Did not witness killing	18	32

Chi-square (p = 0.001)

Externalizing and Internalizing Symptoms and "Emotionality"

Nearly 60 percent had behavioral (or conduct) problems (externalizing symptoms), 40 percent in the moderate or severe range (see table 3–7). Children in foster placements were less likely to have behavioral disturbances, whereas children in children's homes had significantly more (p = 0.015) when compared with children living with relatives of their mother. Which relatives (the father's or mother's) seemed to make little difference for this criterion (see table 3–8). This was statistically significant also when entered into a regression equation with age, sex, and exposure to previous family violence, none of which added to the prediction. Forty percent had neurotic symptoms, such as phobias or obsessions, or mood disorder ("internalizing symptoms") to a moderate or severe extent (table 3–9), with two-thirds judged to be moderately or highly emotional and one-quarter thought to be over-controlled or constricted in their emotional range. Less than

Table 3.7 *Children with Externalizing Symptoms*

Externalizing Symptoms	N	%
Severe	10	11
Moderate	23	26
Mild	19	22
None	36	41

Table 3.8 *The Relationship between the Placement of the Child and Behavioral Disturbance (Externalizing Symptoms)*

Present Placement	No. of Children Showing Externalizing Symptoms	No. of Children Not Showing Externalizing Symptoms
Maternal kin	11	13
Paternal kin	8	5
Foster parents	14	20
Children's home	16	2

Chi-square (p = 0.015)

Table 3.9 *Children with Internalizing Symptoms*

Internalizing Symptoms	N	%
Severe	6	7
Moderate	30	33
Mild	29	32
None	18	20

Table 3.10 *Children's Emotional Range*

Emotionality	N	%
Highly emotional	21	23
Moderately emotional	39	43
Emotional expression in normal range	9	10
Constricted and overcontrolled	21	23

Table 3.11 *The Relationship between the Sex of the Child and Internalizing Symptoms*

	Internalizing Symptoms	No Internalizing Symptoms
Females	29	10
Males	36	20

Chi-square (p = 0.1)

one in ten were thought to have emotions that were normal in both expression and range (see table 3-10). Although almost as many boys as girls were thought of as being more emotional than the average child, there were relatively fewer girls with normal emotional expression. Thus, overall girls are more likely to be highly emotional (p = 0.02). There was a slight trend in this direction too (that is, relatively more girls) for children with "internalizing symptoms" (p = 0.1) (table 3-11). Children with these neurotic symptoms were also more likely to have been exposed to previous interparental violence (again slight trend only, p = 0.1) (table 3-12).

Table 3.12 *The Relationship between Internalizing Symptoms and Previous Exposure to Family Violence*

	Internalizing Symptoms	No Internalizing Symptoms
Family violence	31	17
No family violence	14	3

Chi-square (p = 0.1)

Academic Performance

More than half of our cases had had a noticeable deterioration in their school performance. Only thirteen children (15 percent) continued to do as well after the loss of their parents. One-third had either not started school or could not be assessed because we had insufficient information (see table 3–13).

General Health

One-quarter had health problems that were thought to be psychosomatic.

Identity Problems Related to Aggression and Sexual Drive

Nearly half the children tended to be victimized in their peer groups, with only 15 percent showing persistent aggression or bullying of any significance. Very few showed sexual identity problems, but we would not have expected to elicit any acknowledgment of such problems in an initial assessment interview. In any event it is a problem which would tend to arise later. Nearly one in ten were thought to be false or excessively superficial in their relationships. Although more children who were regarded as excessively passive in their interpersonal relationships came from

Table 3.13 *Children's Academic Performance*

Academic Deterioration	N	%
None	13	15
Some	38	43
Marked	8	9

families in which there had been long-standing violence between the parents, this did not achieve statistical significance (p = 0.17). Boys were as likely to be regarded as passive as girls. Children who were regarded as bullying were no more likely to come from families in which there had been chronic violence, but there were four times as many male bullies as female bullies (p = 0.01).

Attachment Problems

One-quarter of the children were known to have a significant degree of difficulty in their relationships with their attachment figures, indeed in their capacity to attach at all. Over 30 percent were underattached to both their foster mother and father, although for some this may have related more to the brevity of their association than to a more enduring incapacity to form meaningful and secure attachments. Surprisingly few showed anxious insecure patterns of attachment. Forty percent had no discernible attachment problems. Aided mourning (a concept used mainly at the time of assessment implying that the child had participated in funeral rites and/or visited the grave) did not by itself reduce the risk of attachment problems.

Global Measurement of the Extent Versus the Severity of Symptoms

We constructed a global score for each child by adding together each of the subscales' "externalizing symptoms," "internalizing symptoms," "emotionality," "academic performance," general health, and overall attachment problem scores as a rough indication of how *extensively* the child was affected. (This does not necessarily correspond with the severity or intensity of symptoms on the individual subscales. Children scoring high in one category only, for example, may end up with a low global score.) Forty-three children scored 5 or less, forty-seven scored between 6 and 12, and five scored more than 12 out of a possible 17. Only four children had no problems on this scale. In a multivariate analysis the only factors that affected the global score significantly were the placement of the child (children in children's homes were the most extensively affected, p = 0.04) and whether the child had been physically abused in addition to being exposed to chronic violence between the parents (p = 0.06).

CONCLUSIONS

Most of the associations analyzed were not statistically significant. That is not to say that the *factors* we examined were insignificant. Perhaps the most important thing the statistics tell us is that individually the children were in the main more different than they were alike. This is frustrating for the empirical researcher, but for the clinician it is confirmation that sound practice should continue to be rooted in attention to the uniqueness of the child and the particular circumstances. Of course there is some commonality; and the larger the sample, the more feasible it becomes to examine this commonality.

Our future research will benefit from the use of standardized psychometry. With larger numbers there is the possibility of looking for interactions between variables (and not just associations), and we can more easily and usefully compare children seen at similar times after the loss of their parents. With regard to a control group we are considering the value of comparing the children seen as part of this specialized service with children exposed to violence between their parents that has not led to homicide.

Several principles have emerged that guide our treatment of these children.

Principles for Practice

Emergency

1. The children need immediate care in a place that feels safe to them. Caretakers need support and help. Emergency state care may be required.
2. Emergency legal protection should be sought. Children require independent representation and advocacy, and the state should act on their behalf.
3. Health-care services should be placed on alert about the children who will require debriefing, whether or not they saw the killing, and an evaluation concerning the risk they may develop post-traumatic stress disorder should be made. Bereaved relatives also may require urgent help.
4. Expert advice should be sought regarding the planning of contact between children and other key relatives.

Aftermath

1. Planning for the children must begin at once and should not be delayed while the alleged perpetrator of the killing awaits the result of criminal proceedings
2. Emergency arrangements must not be allowed to drift into becoming long-term arrangements without planning.
3. Contact with the father (or mother) and other key relatives is the right of the children and not of the adults concerned. Where conflict arises, this must be the guiding concept for courts and professionals.
4. Therapeutic help should be available to the children and those who care for them.

We have described a study of children whose number increases as we continue our work. They have suffered from the bereavement of a parent compounded by the witnessing of traumatic violence, the arrest or imprisonment or suicide of a parent who has killed, the loss of home, possessions, and neighborhood, and continuing legal insecurity. We are attempting to investigate the effects of these experiences on the children, taking account of their legal framework and identifying their therapeutic needs. We draw on and hope to contribute to the expanding field of knowledge relevant to all child victims of trauma and family violence and those who attempt to provide services for them.

REFERENCES

American Psychiatric Association. (1987). *Diagnostic and Statistical Manual of Mental Disorders*, 3rd ed., revised. Washington, D.C.: American Psychiatric Association.
Ayalon, O. (1983). "Coping with Terrorism." In *Stress Reduction and Prevention*, ed. D. Meichenbaum and M. D. Jeremko. New York: Plenum Press.
Brown, G., and Harris, T. (1978). *The Social Origins of Depression*. London: Tavistock.
Dyregrov, A., and Raundalen, N. (1992). "The Impact of the Gulf War on Children in Iraq." Unpublished.
Garmezy, N., and Rutter, M. (1985). "Acute Reactions to Stress." In *Child and Adolescent Psychiatry: Modern Approaches,* ed. M. Rutter and L. Hersov. London: Blackwell.

Gelles, C. (1990). *Family Violence.* Newbury Park, Calif.: Sage.

Haskey, J. (1991). "Ethnic Minority Populations Resident in Private Households. Estimates by County and Metropolitan Districts of England and Wales." *Population Trends,* 63, HMSO, London.

Hermann, J. L. (1992). *Trauma and Recovery: The Aftermath of Violence from Domestic Abuse to Political Terror.*" New York: Harper Collins.

Jaffe, P. G., Wolfe, D. A., and Wilson, S. K. (1990). "Children of Battered Women." Newbury Park, Calif.: Sage.

Jenkins, J. M., and Smith, M. A. (1991). "Factors Affecting Children Living in Disharmonious Homes: Maternal Reports." *Journal of the American Academy of Child and Adolescent Psychiatry* 29:160–168.

Malmquist, C. (1986). "Children Who Witness Parental Murder: Post Traumatic Aspects." *Journal of the American Academy of Child and Adolescent Psychiatry* 25:370–325.

McFarlane, A. C. (1989). "The Treatment of PTSD." *British Journal of Medical Psychology* 62:81–90.

Norusis, M. J. (1991). SPSS/PC+. Chicago, IL: SPSS INK.

Parry Jones, W. (1992). "The Impact of Disasters on Children and Adolescents." *Young Minds Newsletter* 10:10–12.

Pruett, K. (1979). "Home Treatment of Two Infants Who Witnessed Their Mother's Murder." *Journal of the American Academy of Child and Adolescent Psychiatry* 25:306–319.

Pynoos, R. S., and Eth, S. (1984). "The Child as Witness to Homicide." *Journal of Social Issues* 40:87–108.

—— (1986). "Witness to Violence: The Child Interview." *Journal of the American Academy of Child and Adolescent Psychiatry* 25:306–319.

Raphael, B. (1982). "The Young Child and the Death of a Parent." In *The Place of Attachment in Human Behaviour,* ed. C. M. Parkes and J. Stevenson-Hinde. London: Tavistock.

—— (1992). "Trauma, Loss and Traumatic Loss." Unpublished.

Rosenberg, M. S., and Rossmann, B. B. R. (1990). "The Child Witness to Marital Violence." In *Treatment of Family Violence,* ed. R. T. Ammerman and M. Heisen. New York: Wiley.

Schetky, D. H. (1978). "Pre-schoolers' Response to Murder of Their Mother by Their Fathers. A Study of Four Cases." *Bulletin of the American Academy of Child Psychiatry and the Law* 6:45–47.

Terr, L. C. (1979). "Children of Chowchilla." *Psychoanalytic Study of the Child* 34:547–623.

—— (1983). "Chowchilla Revisited: The Effects of Psychic Trauma Four Years after a School Bus Kidnapping." *American Journal of Psychiatry* 140:1543–1550.

—— (1991). "Childhood Traumas—an Outline and Overview." *American Journal of Psychiatry* 148:10–20.

Walker, L. (1979). *Battered Women.* New York: Harper & Row.

Yule, W., and Udwin, O. (1991). "Screening Child Survivors for Post Traumatic Stress Reactions in Children." *Journal of Traumatic Stress* 3:279–295.

Yule, W., and Williams, R. (1990). "Post Traumatic Stress Reactions in Children." *Journal of Traumatic Stress* 3:229–295.

4

Children of Alcoholic Parents:
At Risk to Experience Violence
and to Develop Violent Behavior

PER-ANDERS RYDELIUS

INTRODUCTION

"Children of Alcoholic Fathers: Their Social Adjustment and Their Health Status over 20 Years" (Rydelius, 1981) presents a review of the literature on children of alcoholics up to 1981. Our work has utilized a computer-based literature search covering Medlars over the period 1940–1993 and continuing through a standing search combination in Medline. A supplementary search of *Psychological Abstracts* and manual searches have supplied additional information.

Since 1973, an increasing number of papers have dealt with problems in children of alcoholics, due mainly to an increasing number of articles on fetal alcohol syndrome (FAS) and the risk to the child if the mother abuses alcohol during pregnancy. However, articles on other aspects of these children's situation and from different scientific disciplines such as general psychiatry, forensic psychiatry, child and adolescent psychiatry, pediatrics, internal medicine, forensic medicine, neurophysiology, neurochemistry, genetics, psychology, pedagogics, and sociology have appeared as well. We found articles written in Czech, English, French, German, Italian, Japanese, Polish, Russian, Swedish, and Spanish, among other languages.

Early reviews in English include El-Guebaly and Offord, 1977, 1979; Ritson, 1975; Warner and Rosett, 1975; Wilson and Orford, 1978. However, we noted that British and American researchers mainly reviewed literature written in English, seldom referring to important studies in other languages. This may be the reason FAS is said to have first been recognized by Ulleland and colleagues (1970) and by Jones and Smith (1973), although a French group reported on "Les enfants de parents alcoöliques. Anomalies observées. A propos de 127 cas" in 1968 (Lemoine et al., 1968). A similar reason may explain why a Polish article (Swiecicki, 1969), using longitudinal and prospective methods to describe the psychosocial development of children from alcoholic and nonalcoholic families, is never referred to in reviews of children of alcoholics.

Although the main research interest in children of alcoholics from 1970 to 1992 seems to have been related either to the effects of FAS or to the risk for these children to develop alcoholism, other consequences have also been discussed. Recently, Sher (1991) stated: "It appears that an adequate scientific explanation of the transmission of risk from alcoholics to their children will require an appreciation of diverse biological, psychological, and sociological factors, and no single vantage point holds a monopoly on the 'truth' " (p. 174). Alcoholism in parents has been looked upon as a possible cause of mental disease or antisocial behavior in their children. Violence against children, severe child abuse, including brain damage and death, child sexual abuse, father-daughter incest, and suicide have been described (Rydelius, 1981).

Investigators interested in the psychopathology of children of alcoholics have found correlations between parental, especially paternal alcoholism and "pathological personality with explosive characteristics" (Shurygin, 1978), "aggressive behavior" (McKenna and Pickens, 1983), and "conduct disorders" (Steinhausen et al., 1984) in children. Many recent publications refer to the multiplicity of problems that children of alcoholics may face. These publications include surveys in the form of symposium papers (e.g., "Children of Alcoholics: An Important Symposium," *British Journal of Addiction* 1988, including papers by Bennett et al., 1988; Blane, 1988; Drake and Vaillant, 1988; Jonsson and Rolf, 1988; Reich et al., 1988; Rolf et al., 1988; Wilson and Nagoshi, 1988; and Woodside, 1988), symposium books (e.g., Robinson and Armstrong, 1988, *Alcohol and Child/Family Health*), special books (e.g., Sher 1991, *Children of Alcoholics: A*

Critical Appraisal of Theory and Research), and annotations (e.g., Knorring, 1991, *Children of Alcoholics*).

In their review El-Guebaly and Offord (1979) state that it is important to acquire a better understanding of so-called competent children who grow up to be well-adjusted individuals despite an environment of grave alcoholism. Using longitudinal and prospective designs for their studies, Rydelius (1981) and Werner (1986) have found and discussed factors relating to sex, personality characteristics, temperament, stressful life events during the first years of life, speech development, and communication skills that may have importance in understanding why some children adjust well and others not, even if they are children from the same family. Sher (1991) concludes: "The parental psychopathology that frequently coexists with parental alcoholism may be a more important determinant of child adjustment than the alcoholism itself; although research has demonstrated a genetic component for alcoholism, environmental factors appear to play an extremely important role in predicting child outcome" (pp. 29, 32).

CHILDREN OF ALCOHOLICS AND THE PROBLEM OF VIOLENCE

Literature surveys indicate that some children of alcoholics suffer from violence of different kinds. They themselves may develop violent behavior; in severe cases, this may include the tendency to assault or rape. Some will be the victims of others' violent behavior, such as physical and sexual abuse; some will develop alcohol abuse, drug abuse, or criminality, also with a high risk of sudden and violent death. Why only some children of alcoholics, even children from the same family, run these risks is not fully known.

However, investigations of children of alcoholics using longitudinal prospective methods indicate that violent behavior in adolescence and adult life is more prevalent in boys from alcoholic families (Nylander and Rydelius, 1982; Rydelius, 1981), and that violent behavior may be the result both of a vulnerable personality and of violence experienced during infancy and childhood. Perhaps violent behavior of this kind is the result of a "social" inheritance transferred from father to son. This paper will discuss this possibility from a Swedish perspective, using both theoretical approaches and empirical data.

In child psychiatric research in Sweden, the alcoholic family has been looked upon as a model for investigations into childhood psychopathology and its consequences for adult life (Nylander, 1960). From an early time, researchers in Sweden favored using longitudinal and prospective research strategies aimed at the early detection and future prevention of violent behavior, juvenile delinquency, alcohol and drug abuse, and sudden violent death in children and youth. This is closely related to the development of child and adolescent psychiatry in Sweden as an independent academic and medical discipline.

The prospective long-term follow-up of children treated at child guidance clinics in Stockholm started in the 1950s and presented detailed follow-ups after ten and twenty years (Curman and Nylander, 1976; Nylander, 1979). The results show that children from homes where the parents are alcoholics or have mental problems of other kinds do not finish treatment and run severe risks for future maladjustment. The reasons for treatment failure seem to be related to a lack of motivation among the parents.

In 1947, the Stockholm Child Welfare Board opened the Children's Village of Skå, a treatment home for deviant children (Madsen, 1982). In 1967, Gustav Jonsson, director of the home from its beginning until he retired, presented his thesis, "Delinquent Boys, Their Parents and Grandparents" (Jonsson, 1967), in which he proposed a theory of "social" inheritance, or transfer of maladaptive behavior from one generation to the other.

At the beginning of this century, Swedish professors and chairmen of psychiatry attempted to develop specific knowledge about the early symptoms of psychotic disorders. Due to this interest and the inspiration of the mental health movement of the 1920s, Swedish child psychiatry also had an origin within psychiatry. In 1947, at the universities of Uppsala and Lund, child and adolescent psychiatric wards and clinics opened within the departments of psychiatry. A scientific contribution to the field from the 1940s is the thesis by Edith Otterström, "Delinquency and Children from Bad Homes" (Otterström, 1946), which discusses the influence of parental alcoholism on children.

The Implications of History for Child Psychiatric Research

Child and adolescent psychiatry in Sweden developed from different disciplines within the medical and behavioral sciences, all needing knowledge about normal and deviant development and the behavior of children. The most important sources were pediatrics, psychiatry, psychology, education, sociology, and social welfare. From the outset, this historical background also led to multidisciplinary cooperation and planning for Swedish child psychiatric research in order to examine different possibilities from different scientific frames of reference.

The late Sven Ahnsjö (1906–1992) became the first professor and chairman of child and adolescent psychiatry in Sweden. In 1941, he defended his thesis, "Delinquency in Girls and Its Prognosis" (Ahnsjö, 1941), and became the most important proponent of the concept that child and adolescent psychiatry should become a discipline of its own. He held the chair at the Karolinska Institute from 1958 to 1972 and had a broad education and experience from fields including genetics, pediatrics, psychiatry, school mental health consultation, and his work on child social welfare committees. Although his scientific training was in genetics, the results of his research indicated that a multidisciplinary view and a social psychiatric perspective concerning child psychiatric research was needed. His opinions greatly influenced research activities until today.

However, the history of the development of Swedish child and adolescent psychiatry as a medical and academic discipline also points to another important consequence for research. Current knowledge has been achieved mainly by two methods, the retrospective "anamnestic" method and the prospective "descriptive" method.

From psychiatry and psychoanalysis child and adolescent psychiatry inherited a retrospective view of deviant behavior and psychiatric disorders. Through the case history with the adult patient, the psychiatrist tries to identify important factors that preceded the problem. This retrospective technique has raised a number of questions. The main problem is that the *prospective/developmental perspective* is lost, and the question arises when during maturation and development childhood psychopathology can be described by terminology taken from adult psychiatry. An example of this problem was the introduction of the term *infantile autism* in an era when psychopathologic terminology from adults conventionally was used to describe psychopathology in children as well. In 1973, at his retirement, the American child psychiatrist Leo Kanner (1973) discussed this in his book *Childhood Psychosis–Initial Studies and New Insights*. He recalls how he chose the term *autism* to indicate a psychopathologic disturbance of affective contact in a small child when he first described the syndrome. Educated in Europe, he learned that autism was a symptom of schizophrenia; at first he thought that the children he described might have symptoms similar to those of adult schizophrenic patients. His further studies indicated that this was not the case, and he regretted the use of adult psychiatric psychopathologic terminology to designate a childhood symptom.

Another problem is that sex differences are not obvious when retrospective methods are used. In child psychiatric research investigators often study children as a group instead of studying boys and girls separately. The roots of Swedish child psychiatry within pediatrics gave researchers in the discipline alternative, prospective approaches to the study of development and maturation from birth to adulthood. Pediatricians were interested in following such variables as weight and height in boys and girls separately over time; these prospective methods influenced the early Swedish child psychiatrists to follow child psychiatric problems by prospective methods, as well with boys and girls separated, observing the developing children from an early age.

Following the development of children from birth to adulthood by prospective longitudinal methods generates a research problem that is not apparent in retrospectively designed studies: that is, the observation time will be at least twenty years. The results from the so-called Lundby study in Sweden (Hagnell et al., 1990) indicate that an observation time of around forty years is needed to study such events as the incidence of criminality and alcohol abuse in the general population. So far, it has been possible to compensate for the generational shift among active researchers in child psychiatry, so that ongoing prospective longitudinal studies have been continued.

STUDIES OF CHILDREN OF ALCOHOLIC PARENTS

In the 1950s Ingvar Nylander, (professor of child and adolescent psychiatry in Umeå from 1966 to 1972, and successor to Sven Ahnsjö as professor and chairman of child and adolescent psychiatry at the Karolinska Institute from 1972 to 1988), studied childhood psychopathology from a prospective perspective using multidisciplinary methods. He started from a biological point of view, including the possibilities of brain damage and brain dysfunction, to explain psychopathologic symptoms in children.

He conducted studies on psychopathology in children, investigating patients seen through consultation on the medical and surgical wards at Crown Princess Lovisa's Children's Hospital, and published *Physical Symptoms and Psychogenic Etiology: An Investigation of Consultation Material* (Nylander, 1959) and a description of the clinical investigation of children who had suffered from meningoencephalitis, *Sequele* of *Primary Aseptic Meningo-Encephalitis"* (Müller et al., 1958). Nylander found support for psychosocial factors rather than biological factors to explain common child psychiatric symptoms.

These findings led him to advance a hypothesis concerning the relationship between the mental health of parents and nervous symptoms in their children: "Children who live under stress due to serious emotional disturbances in the home may, as a result, react with nonorganic physical symptoms. As a result, these children come up, either too late or perhaps not at all for psychiatric assessment and treatment. Instead they look for help from outpatient departments or hospitals for physical diseases, and in many cases, the true nature of the symptoms never comes to light" (p. 10).

To test his hypothesis Nylander (1960) considered several types of parental mental problems as subjects of investigation and finally chose the environment of the chronic alcoholic. "Only the chronic alcoholic's children could be said, with a high degree of certainty, to have lived under emotional stress so long that this stress could be thought to have prejudiced the children's mental health" (p. 11). When testing his hypothesis on children of alcoholic fathers, Nylander used a study design in which the experimental subjects were matched with controls, and boys and girls were studied separately.

Nylander found that children of alcoholic fathers were neglected and presented psychiatric symptoms more often than controls. Some children showed somatic symptoms such as headache, fatigue, abdominal pain, nausea, vomiting, and "growing pains."

Others showed symptoms of emotional lability, anxiety, depression, and sleep disorders. Another group showed difficulties in concentration, motor restlessness, aggressive behavior, and interpersonal difficulties. Fifty percent of the children from alcoholic homes, compared with 10 percent of the controls, had problems adjusting in school although they were of normal intelligence. Nylander also found sex differences. In girls, the symptom frequency rose with increasing age. Encopresis, speech disorders, and motor restlessness were seen more often in boys, while abdominal pain was recorded more often in girls.

Nylander also investigated the psychiatric status of the mothers. In Sweden the prevalence of alcoholism among women was low from the 1920s to the 1960s owing to temperance laws. This may explain why only 2 of 141 wives of severe male alcoholics investigated were themselves alcoholics. However, Nylander found that these women were often tired and showed "psychic insufficiency"; he described them as "worn out," as a secondary effect of their husbands' alcoholism. He looked upon a "worn out" mother as another emotional stressor for the child, perhaps also indicating that that mother was unable to protect and support the child.

In a twenty-year follow-up of the same children using data on registered social adjustment and health from childhood to adulthood, Rydelius (1981) found that compared with controls children of alcoholic fathers have a higher risk of developing alcohol and drug abuse and criminality and have a higher need for somatic and psychiatric health care. Boys from alcoholic homes had been admitted to hospitals because of accidental poisoning, attempted suicide, and injuries due to accidents or assault more often than boys from control families. A similiar tendency, although not significant, was found among girls from alcoholic homes.

There were important sex differences concerning social adjustment. While girls from alcoholic homes adjusted socially almost as well as control girls, one in four boys from alcoholic homes (compared to only 5 percent of the controls) was a "social wreck" twenty years later. Girls from alcoholic homes suffered from gynecological problems more often than controls.

Statistically confirmed relationships between subgroups of boys from alcoholic homes indicated that boys whose behavior was characterized by aggressive acting out in childhood later developed serious social adjustment problems, including criminality and alcohol and drug abuse, in comparison with boys whose reaction pattern in childhood expressed a more introverted anxiety, exhibited as symptoms of neurotic anxiety, headaches, abdominal pains, or heart trouble. The boys acting out aggressively also seemed to be biologically late developers, with immature speech during early childhood. The criminality shown by the alcoholic boys often included violent behavior. Robbery, armed robbery, assault, rape, drunk driving, and manslaughter were found. Such criminality was seldom seen among control boys.

The following case history illustrates the development from childhood to adulthood of the son of an alcoholic father:

> He was a male, 26 years of age and the third of five siblings. The alcoholic father behaved in a disorderly manner during drinking periods. The mother abused alcohol and drugs. The family was under the surveillance of the Temperance Board. When the boy was investigated at the age of 6 he showed signs of neglect and aggressive behavior. At follow-up he had not married and had no children. He changed his place of residence thirteen times from the age of 6 to 26. He was known in the registers of the Child Welfare Committee, because of juvenile delinquency. At the age of 17 he was also noted in the Criminal Register. After that time he had sixteen notations concerning crimes, including robbery and assault. He was sentenced by a court on eight occasions, and was once sent to prison. In the Temperance registers he was known since the age of 16, for alcohol and drug abuse. He required surgical treatment on twenty-four occasions, seven times because of injuries due to assault. He required medical care on twenty-two occasions and was a patient in a child and adolescent psychiatric unit, a clinic for alcohol treatment, and a psychiatric clinic. During his visits to hospitals for medical, surgical, or mental treatment he was noted as drunk on twenty-one occasions. Seven times he was admitted for poisoning, each time due to an attempted suicide.

In another study, Nylander and Rydelius (1982) compared children of alcoholic fathers from excellent social conditions (the fathers were doctors, dentists, lawyers, managing directors, etc.) to those from poor social conditions. The results indicated that regardless of social background, children are at risk to develop criminality and alcohol and drug abuse if the father is an alcoholic.

These relationships among the home situation, childhood psychopathology, and later deviant behavior have been examined in several independent longitudinal prospective studies of both selected groups and groups from the general population. The children of alcoholic parents, young alcohol abusers, children attending child and adolescent psychiatric in- or outpatient departments, children attending pediatric surgery departments, and youngsters from probationary schools have been the subjects of studies of the possible relationships between the parents' mental health and the subsequent adjustment of their children, including the risk of a sudden and violent death (Rydelius, 1983a).

The investigations utilized interviews, questionnaires, psychometric tests, and register data as well as physiological and biochemical data in order to describe the child and his/her situation at a certain time. Prospective follow-up assessments at regular intervals measured the outcome. In our samples the outcomes examined such factors as criminality, alcohol and drug abuse, and psychiatric or somatic illness. Interviews, questionnaires, and register data also have been used to measure outcome, at intervals of 5, 10, 15, 20, 25, and 30 years.

HYPOTHESES: THE DEVELOPMENT OF CHILDREN OF ALCOHOLIC PARENTS

Results of prospective studies of selected groups and of teenage boys from the general population (Nylander and Rydelius, 1973, 1979; Rydelius, 1983b,c) supported the hypothesis that young male alcohol abusers were often the children of alcoholic parents, were identified early as "problematic," and were often known as criminals. From these studies the following hypothesis was put forward:

The problem of impulsivity — a lack of self-control — which can be seen in young adults with violent behavior is perhaps a continuation of the same personality factors that can be seen in growing children, giving rise to both impulsiveness and aggressive acting-out behavior. Maybe impulsiveness and aggressive acting-out behavior develop in genetically vulnerable boys growing up in homes afflicted by psychosocial stress factors such as alcohol and drug abuse and/or violent behavior in the parents. Even when very small, these vulnerable boys react to the poor circumstances and the violence by the parents with early motoric restlessness and impulsive and aggressive behavior, whereas other boys, even brothers, may react with depression or anxiety of an "introvert" type to the same kind of stress. As a consequence of their aggressive, violent behavior these vulnerable boys experience problems in relation [ships], being repelled by "normal" children, and therefore seek the company of friends in similar situations. In this group of "bad" friends they soon find that sniffing glue, [or using] alcohol or drugs will either give anxiety relief or a kick. . . . [T]his leads to a daily use of the intoxicant and to a still worse adjustment and ultimately into early alcohol and drug abuse and delinquency. [Rydelius 1983c, p. 384]

Research on children at risk also indicates a possible link between parental mental health, childhood symptoms, delinquent behavior, and a high risk of death before the age of 24 years because of suicide or accident. A longitudinal prospective study of teenagers admitted to the Swedish probationary schools in 1967 revealed that 13 percent of the boys and 10 percent of the girls had died by the end of 1985, owing to suicide or violent death, often related to alcohol and drug abuse. The death expectancy of healthy Swedish boys and girls in corresponding age groups during the same period of time is 1.2–3.1 percent and 1.1–2.6 percent, respectively (Rydelius, 1988).

The life history of a 17-year-old boy who died from a sudden violent death illustrates the results of the research:

Age

At birth	A sociopathic, alcoholic father
3	Divorce, after father violated and abused mother
5	Mother remarried new alcoholic male
6	New divorce; boy aggressive in preschool
8	School problems, aggressive behavior
9	Mother at a psychiatric hospital due to alcohol and drug abuse

10	Pilfering, glue sniffing, severe disciplinary problems at school
12	Mother committed suicide; boy caught stealing
13	Hospitalized because of alcohol intoxication
15	Assaulted another person using a knife; alcohol and drug abuse; probationary school
17	Dead in car crash; single accident; alcohol intoxication at autopsy

Studies of children of alcoholic parents further indicate that boys and girls differ considerably concerning the risk for future "bad" behavior. Differences in childhood psychopathology and development between and within the sexes have been found that may explain such different outcomes. Examples of this are findings indicating that vulnerable boys, in whom immaturity and aggressive acting-out behavior appear in early childhood, constitute the group with the highest risk to develop severe social maladjustment, including violent behavior in their teens.

The theoretical and empirical background for the assumption of a link between the emotional stress of being the child of an alcoholic parent and the appearance of psychopathology in the child has been developed further in other studies (Rydelius, 1981, 1983a,b,c). Several principles emerge from this research. Irrespective of whether a specific psychopathology or personality type and/or genetic or biological vulnerability leads to alcoholism, the alcoholic him- or herself will develop psychopathology secondary to the alcoholism. These symptoms are of two different kinds in relation to time. One type of symptom develops gradually over the years and eventually shows itself through the typical clinical picture of chronic alcoholism. At this stage of alcoholism, the problem is often obvious to others, such as friends, neighbors, companions, and colleagues at work. Other symptoms show themselves earlier, before the alcoholism becomes obvious to people outside the family. These symptoms include the mood changes secondary to intoxication and the developing alcoholism. They encompass sudden mood swings, a bad temper, acting-out behavior, angry outbursts, aggressiveness, violence, and unpredictible behavior during drunkenness. Alternatively, they include depressive behavior with a tendency to cry, be dependent, or "be sick" during drunkenness. Difficult behavior during hangovers and other typical problems complete the picture. More and more of the family's money is needed to cover the expense of the alcoholic's wine, beer, or liquor, sometimes bringing the family to poverty. Moreover, the impulsivity and unpredictable behavior of the alcoholic parent put the children at risk to become victims of violence or to be witnesses of violence when they see a drunken father beat up their mother or sexually abuse her.

Boys who are genetically "programmed" for immature and slow mental development, including immature language development and a tendency to react to stress with impulsive behavior and motoric restlessness, react to this family situation by showing aggressive acting-out behavior. They "learn" to fight instead of to solve problems by the use of language as they identify with their violent fathers. These aggressive boys are not met with empathy from persons outside their families, making their situation even worse as they are looked upon as "bad" boys. Their brothers and sisters who are "programmed" for average development will instead react with anxiety, sadness, and crying and seek comfort with the help of their language skills. These children may perhaps be even more resilient as they meet with empathy from friends, teachers, and relatives. If this is so, it may explain how violence within the family may promote violent behavior in vulnerable children, but not in all children in the same family.

The kind of late and immature development described among boys with an alcoholic father is probably a normal variant of male development, also found in boys from healthy and well-functioning homes. From clinical experience, it seems that well-functioning parents support their immature boys in many ways: they do not impose additional stress or demands on them. Comments such as "Boys in our family develop late," "His father acted the same way when he was a child," "He acts like this when he is tired," and so on, indicate that the parents meet such boys with understanding and empathy. The boy's tendency to be impulsive and to show motoric overactivity is often compensated by special efforts from the parents. During his maturation, his tendency to react with impulsivity and overactivity fades away and is of minor importance when he is a grown-up. A good "social" inheritance exists.

A similar chain of events may lead to the result that some girls in violent families learn, by identification with their mothers, to be nonaggressive and to be beaten. As their parents' sexual life is influenced by the violent behavior of their father, these girls may choose an alcoholic male as their husband, and are themselves beaten up and sexually abused in marriage. Perhaps the nonaggressive behavior of these girls also results in alcohol problems being hidden for a longer time than those of boys, whose behavior makes their alcohol problems obvious to friends, police, and society. If this is the case, the search for sex-specific "female psychopathology" must be more extensive, starting with infant girls.

The findings from our research and that of others (e.g. Jonsson's prospective follow-ups of delinquent boys [Andersson et al., 1976], Jonsson's theory on "social inheritance," and Bohman's [1970] investigations of adoptive children and his genetic studies on criminality and abuse [1978]) support this theory of both a genetic and a social inheritance (including psychological factors) in the explanation of how violent behavior develops from infancy into adult life. Similar results were found in psychological longitudinal research in Sweden by Lie (1981) and by Olweus (1980), the Magnusson group (Stattin, 1989), and the Schalling group (Klinteberg et al., 1992) from the Department of Psychology at Stockholm University.

A hypothesis describing how the development of juvenile delinquency, early drug and alcohol abuse, and the risk of a sudden violent death can be traced by pediatricians, child health nurses, teachers, and school psychiatrists has been proposed on the basis of the empirical data produced by the above-mentioned studies (Nylander, 1981). This hypothesis is now being tested in a new longitudinal prospective study of a birth cohort of children from the general population (Nylander and Zetterström, 1983) followed from the beginning of pregnancy.

Some 532 pregnant women who lived in a Stockholm suburb and visited their maternity center for the first time during their pregnancies agreed to take part in the study. Their mental health and psychosocial situation and those of their husbands, their pregnancies, and their deliveries were subsequently studied. Of these women, 498 gave birth to 501 children, including three pairs of twins. All but four of these children remained alive after three months and comprise the study group. The development and health of these children have been followed with home visits at 3 weeks of age, at 1 and 4 years, before starting school, and currently, when they have attended school for two or more years and are 10–11 years of age. More than 80 percent of the cohort still participate. Results from this study support the hypothesis that there are differences between boys and girls in mental development. Moreover, boys seem to be more sensitive to poor psychosocial conditions in the home (Nordberg et al., 1991).

In this study of children from the general population, 12 percent of the children were born to families in which either the father, the mother, or both were known to be alcoholics or alcohol abusers. Recently published results show that the children of alcoholics have a significantly higher risk of pre- and postnatal death and have poorer mental development and more childhood psychopathology than other children. Boys from alcoholic families, more often than other boys, show aggressive behavior or temper tantrums and violence against other persons (Nordberg et al., 1993). These findings support Nylander's 1960 findings and also the hypothesis put forward above concerning the development of aggressive behavior.

CONCLUSIONS

The results of prospective longitudinal investigations of the development of childhood psychopathology, using children of alcoholics as a model, indicate that the development of violent behavior may be the result of both a genetic vulnerability and a social inheritance. The genetic vulnerability may be a constitutional developmental factor, which, although it is a variant of normal development, shows itself as a delayed and immature development from birth to adulthood, including a tendency to react to stress by impulsivity and acting-out behavior. The social inheritance may be the violence experienced in the family, through which the boy learns to meet other people with aggressive and violent behavior.

REFERENCES

Ahnsjö, S. (1941). "Delinquency in Girls and Its Prognosis." *Acta Paediatrica Scandinavica*, suppl. no. 3.

Aichorn, A. (1925) 1951. *Verwahrloste Jugend.* Bern: Verlag Hans Huber.

Andersson, M., Jonsson, G., and Kälvesten, A.-L. (1976). *Stockholm*

Boys, Normal and delinquents in the 1950's— What Happened? Stockholm: Rosenlundstryckeriet. In Swedish.

Bauman, P., and Levine, S. (1986). "The Development of Children of Drug Addicts." *International Journal of the Addictions* 21:849–863.

Bennet, L., Wolin, S., and Reiss, D. (1988). "Deliberate Family Process: A Strategy for Protecting Children of Alcoholics." *British Journal of Addiction* 83:821–829.

Blane, H. (1988). "Prevention Issues with Children of Alcoholics." *British Journal of Addiction* 83:793–798.

Bohman, M. (1970). *Adopted Children and Their Families: A Follow-up Study of Adopted Children, Their Background, Environment and Adjustment.* Stockholm: Proprius.

_____ (1978). "Some Genetic Aspects of Alcoholism and Criminality." *Archives of General Psychiatry* 35:269–276.

Curman, H., and Nylander, I. (1976). "A 10-year Prospective Follow-up Study of 2268 Cases at the Child Guidance Clinics in Stockholm." *Acta Psychiatr Scandinavica*, suppl. no. 260.

Drake, R., and Vaillant, G. (1988). "Predicting Alcoholism and Personality Disorder in a 33-Year Longitudinal Study of Children of Alcoholics." *British Journal of Addiction* 83:799–807.

El-Guebaly, N., and Offord, D. R. (1977). "The Offspring of Alcoholics. A Critical Review." *American Journal of Psychiatry* 134:357–365.

_____ (1979). "On Being the Offspring of an Alcoholic. An Update." *Alcoholism* 3:148–157.

Edwards, G. (1988). "Children of Alcoholics: An Important Symposium." *British Journal of Addiction* 83:783.

Fried, I. (1992). "The Mellansjö School and Treatment Home. Stockholm: Gotab. In Swedish.

Gunnarson, S. (1946). "Some Types of Nervous Disorders in Children and Their Prognosis." *Acta Paediatrica Scandinavica*, suppl. no. 4.

Hagnell, O., Essen-Möller, E., Lanke, J., et al. (1990). *The Incidence of Mental Illness over a quarter of a Century.* Stockholm: Almqvist & Wiksell International.

Johnson, J., and Rolf, J. (1988) "Cognitive Functioning in Children from Alcoholic and Non-alcoholic Families." *British Journal of Addiction* 83:849–857.

Jones, K. L., and Smith D. N. (1973). "Recognition of the Fetal Alcohol Syndrome in Early Infancy. *Lancet* 2:999–1001.

Jonsson, G. (1967). "Delinquent Boys, Their Parents and Grandparents." *Acta Psychiatrica Scandinavica*, suppl. no. 195.

Jundell, I. (1915). *Broken Minds.* Stockholm: Barnens Dagblad. In Swedish.

Kanner, L. (1973). *Childhood Psychosis: Initial Studies and New Insights.* Washington, D.C.: V. H. Winston & Sons.

Key, E. (1909). *The Century of the Child.* London: G. P. Putnam's Sons.

Klinteberg, B., Humble, K., and Schalling, D. (1992). "Personality and Psychopathy of Males with a History of Early Criminal Behaviour." *European Journal of Personality* 6:245–266.

Lemoine, P., Harousseau, H., Bortreyru, J.-P., et al. (1968). "Les enfants de parents alcooliques. Anomalies observées. Apropos de 127 cas." Paris: *Quest. Médical* 25:476–482.

Lie, N. (1981). "Young Law-Breakers. A Prospective-Longitudinal Study." *Acta Paediatrica Scandinavica*, suppl. no. 288.

Madsen, K. (1982). "A Site Visit to the Family Village at Skå-Edeby in Stockholm." In *The Child in His Family: Children in Turmoil: Tomorrow's Parents*, vol. 7, ed. J. Anthony and C. Chiland, New York: Wiley, 181–184.

McKenna, T., and Pickens, R. (1983). "Personality Characteristics of Alcoholic Children of Alcoholics." *Journal of Studies on Alcohol* 44:688–700.

Müller, R., Nylander, I., Larsson, L.-E., et al. (1958). "Sequelae of Primary Aseptic Meningo-Encephalitis. A Clinical, Sociomedical, Electroencephalographic and Psychological Study." *Acta Psychiatrica et Neurologica Scandinavica*, suppl. no. 126.

Neill, A. S. (1925). *The Problem Child*. London: Jenkins.

Nordberg, L., Rydelius, P.-A., and Zetterström, R. (1991). "Psycho-motor and Mental Development from Birth to Age of Four Years; Sex Differences and Their Relation to Home Environment." *Acta Paediatrica Scandinavica*, suppl. no. 378.

_____ (1993). "Children of Alcoholic Parents: Health, Growth, Mental Development and Psychopathology until School Age. Results from a Prospective Longitudinal Study of Children from the General Population. *Acta Paediatrica Scandinavica*, Suppl. no. 387.

Nylander, I. (1959). "Physical Symptoms and Psychogenic Etiology. An Investigation of Consultation Material." *Acta Paediatrica Scandinavica*, suppl. no. 117:69–77.

_____ (1960). "Children of Alcoholic Fathers." *Acta Paediatrica Scandinavica*, Suppl. no. 121.

_____ (1979). "A 20-year Prospective Follow-up Study of 2164 Cases at the Child Guidance Clinics in Stockholm." *Acta Paediatrica Scandinavica*, suppl. no. 276.

_____ (1981). "The Development of Antisocial Behaviour in Children. *Acta Paedopsychiatrica* 47:71–80.

Nylander I., and Rydelius P.-A. (1973). "The Relapse of Drunkenness in Non-asocial Teen-age Boys. *Acta Psychiatrica Scandinavica* 49:435–443.

_____ (1979). "Drunkenness in Children and Teen-agers." *International Journal of Mental Health* 7:117–131.

_____ (1982). "A Comparison between Children of Alcoholic Fathers from Excellent versus Poor Social Conditions." *Acta Paediatrica Scandinavica* 71:809–813.

Nylander, I., Rydelius P.-A., Nordberg, L., et al. (1989). "Infant Health and Development in Relation to the Family Situation." *Acta Paediatrica Scandinavica* 78:1–10.

Nylander, I., and Zetterström, R. (1983). "Home Environment of Children in a New Stockholm Suburb. A Prospective Longitudinal Study." *Acta Paediatrica Scandinavica*, suppl. no. 310.

Olweus, D. (1980). "Familial and Temperamental Determinants of Aggressive Behavior in Adolescent Boys: A Causal Analysis." *Developmental Psychology* 16:644–660.

Otterström, E. (1946). "Delinquency and Children from Bad Homes." *Acta Paediatrica Scandinavica*, suppl. no. 5.

Reich, W., Earls, F., and Powell, J. (1988). "A Comparison of the Home and Social Environments of Children of Alcoholic and Non-alcoholic Parents." *British Journal of Addiction* 83:831–839.

Ritson, B. (1975). "Children and Alcohol." *Child Care Health Development* 1:263–269.

Robinson, G., and Armstrong, R., eds. (1988). *Alcohol and Child/Family Health, 1988. A Conference with Particular Reference to the Prevention of Alcohol-Related Birth Defects.* B. C. FAS Resource Group. Vancouver, British Columbia V5M 3E8, Canada.

Rolf, J., Johnson, J., Israel, E., et al. (1988). "Depressive Affect in School-Aged Children of Alcoholics." *British Journal of Addiction* 83:841–848.

Rydelius, P.-A. (1981). "Children of Alcoholic Fathers. Their Social Adjustment and Their Health Status over 20 Years." *Acta Paediatrica Scandinavica*, suppl. no. 286.

――――― (1983a). "Alcohol and Family Life." *Child Health* 2:76–85.

――――― (1983b). "Alcohol-Abusing Teenage Boys. Testing a Hypothesis on the Relationship between Alcohol Abuse and Social Background Factors, Criminality and Personality in Teenage Boys." *Acta Psychiatrica Scandinavica* 68:368–380.

――――― (1983c). "Alcohol-Abusing Teenage Boys. Testing a Hypothesis on Alcohol Abuse and Personality Factors, Using a Personality Inventory." *Acta Psychiatrica Scandinavica* 68:381–385.

――――― (1988). "The Development of Antisocial Behaviour and Sudden Violent Death." *Acta Psychiatrica Scandinavica* 77:398–403.

Sher, K. J. (1991). *Children of Alcoholics. A Critical Appraisal of Theory and Research.* Chicago: University of Chicago Press.

Shurygin, G. E. (1978). "Psychogenic Pathologic Personality Formation in Children and Adolescents with Alcoholic Fathers. *Zhurnal Nevropatologii Psikiatrii* 78:1566–1569. In Russian.

Stattin, H., and Magnusson, D. (1989). "The Role of Early Aggressive

Behavior in the Frequency, Seriousness, and Type of Later Crime." *Journal of Consulting and Clinical Psychology* 57:710–718.

Steinhausen, H.-C., Göbel, D., and Nestler, V. (1984). "Psychopathology in the Offspring of Alcoholic Parents." *Journal of the American Academy of Child Psychiatry* 23:465–471.

Swiecicki, A. (1969). "Adult Adjustment of Children from Alcoholic and Non-alcoholic Families." *Problemy Alkoholizmu* (Warsawa) 17:1–7. In Polish.

Ulleland, C., Wennberg, R. P., Igo, P., et al. (1970). "The Offspring of Alcoholic Mothers." *Paediatric Research* 4:474.

Von Knorring, A.-L. (1991). "Annotation: Children of Alcoholics." *Journal of Child Psychology and Psychiatry* 32:411–421.

Warner, R., and Rosett, H. (1975). "The Effects of Drinking in Offspring. An Historical Survey of the American and British Literature." *Journal of Studies on Alcohol* 36:1395–1420.

Werner, E. (1986). "Resilient Offspring of Alcoholics: A Longitudinal Study from Birth to Age 18." *Journal of Studies on Alcohol* 47:34–40.

Wilson, C., and Orford, J. (1978). "Children of Alcoholics." *Journal of Studies on Alcohol* 39:121–142.

Wilson, J., and Nagoshi, C. (1988). "Adult Children of Alcoholics: Cognitive and Psychomotor Characteristics." *British Journal of Addiction* 83:809–820.

Woodside, M. (1988). "Research on Children of Alcoholics: Past and Future." *British Journal of Addiction* 83:785–792.

5

Treating Aggressive Children through Residential Treatment

YECHESKIEL COHEN

INTRODUCTION: SEVERE CHILDHOOD AGGRESSION, RESIDENTIAL TREATMENT, AND "CONTAINMENT"

The aim of this chapter is to describe the treatment of aggressive children through long-term residential treatment. Extensive research has enabled clinicians to classify childhood disturbances into conduct disorders, affective disorders, learning difficulties, developmental disturbances, and other diagnostic categories (King and Noshpitz, 1991). But aggression as a symptom crosses diagnostic categories and confronts the treatment staff with severe challenges for coping; we often refer to these children as "aggressive children" no matter to which diagnostic category they "belong." When we face severely aggressive children we find that in most of the cases the aggression is a phenomenon that lies in the family and is transmitted from one generation to the other. It is our belief that the most troubled children carry this aggression with them from infancy and that their disturbance is the outcome of multiple causes. All kinds of treatment methods, be they behavior modification or medication or various kinds of individual or group therapy, fail to change the vicious circle of aggression. Residential treatment encompasses the entire personality and temporarily puts it in abeyance from reality, so it can be the only way to bring about crucial and permanent changes.

TREATING AGGRESSIVE CHILDREN

Treating aggressive children in residential centers poses difficult and complicated issues for staff. Placed in residential treatment after having been in various kinds of treatment frameworks — whether clinics and special education classes while at home, or boarding schools and/or foster care after being removed from their homes — these children are "well experienced" in a wide spectrum of reactions to their aggressive behavior. Moreover, their clinical status may deteriorate as an outcome of rejection from various placements. The main concern of residential treatment therefore should be *containing* (Bion, 1984) aggressive reactions, antagonism, and oppositional behavior. By containment we do not mean just calming or diminishing the aggressive symptoms, whether by medication or other disciplinary methods, especially since these children experienced such interventions prior to being placed in residential treatment.

Unless we are able to contain the aggressive reactions and behaviors, the children will continue relating to others as the target of their projections. For example, they may regard care workers as "bad," as "always" preferring others, as "always" hitting and depriving them of any source of satisfaction. There is no possibility getting out of this projective relationship through the use of cognitive and rational argumentation such as "But don't you see that just a minute ago I brought you . . . " This kind of argument is suitable for children who are able to "use" others, whose capacity for differentiation from the principal others in their lives is healthy. The aggressive children we refer to here lack the ability to differentiate, which explains why the borders between them and others are often blurred. This handicap also finds expression in their cognitive behavior, hindering their ability to think objectively and rationally.

Two case vignettes illustrate the manner in which one should contain the child's aggression. The first vignette is taken from a therapeutic session.

After a long period of time in which the child had regarded the therapist as an ideal person, in contrast to all his other staff caretakers, the child suddenly told the therapist that he was just like all the other people in the center after all. "You are against me all the time, just like all the rest." The therapist did not ask the child for an explanation, nor did he try to prove that he had always protected the child. On the contrary, the therapist "accepted" this feeling and said to the child: "It must be very difficult for you to come to the session today when you sense in me someone who is opposed to you." The child reacted by taking a ball and asking the therapist to play with him. Later on, he complained about an incident he had had in the dining room. He could do this because the therapist had contained the child's hostile feeling.

The second vignette is taken from a daily scene in the dining hall.

Danny entered the hall shouting and running. When he saw his child-care worker from a distance he threw a chair and then went to his seat. He continued to shout and curse several kids around him, which in turn created total bedlam in the dining hall, as one of the kids approached Danny and tried to hit him. The care worker quickly went over and fetched Danny, taking him forcefully out of the dining hall. Danny tried to break free of the care worker's hands, kicking him, cursing, and crying loudly. The care worker did not talk too much while holding him but just said over and over again: "I am here to protect you no matter what you say about me, and I know that right now you must hate me very much." Later on, the care worker took him into a room nearby so that they could be alone. As Danny calmed down a bit the care worker said to him that it seemed that something must have hurt him terribly and whenever he was ready to tell him what happened, the care worker would be willing to listen. Then he added: "Anyway, I won't let you go now unless I am sure that you are safe, and if you prefer to eat here in this room now, then I will bring the food here; but if you feel you can eat with the other kids then we will both go back to the dining hall." Danny preferred to eat with all the other kids. Later in the evening before bedtime the care worker went to Danny's bed and they reconstructed the scene step by step.

This vignette illustrates an everyday occurrence in residential treatment centers where most of the children are violent and aggressive. Even in such public places as dining halls the staff should find the right ways to contain the aggression of the children in order to bring about an essential change not only in the children's behavior, but in their overall personalities.

These vignettes point to some of the reasons why long-term residential treatment is the treatment of choice for very aggressive children.

LONG-TERM RESIDENTIAL TREATMENT CENTERS

It is our belief—and experience—that children such as those described in the above vignettes need a totally different therapeutic approach than that usually administered. The usual assumption is that a child who has suffered from a harmful early childhood needs a healthy substitute family in order to provide him with what he lacks to facilitate healthy development. However, repeated failure to cure these children through foster care or short-term residential treatment proves that, unfortunately, these severely disturbed children need something different. They need to be disentangled from the unhealthy relationship in which they are enmeshed with their primary caretakers. They need an environment that will allow them to establish their own integrated and cohesive selves.

Since the 1930s clinicians throughout the world have tried to create therapeutic environments specially suited for the intensive, long-term treatment of children with serious emotional disorders. These residential programs have provided therapy and at the same time have served as clinical laboratories for studying children's inner lives and behavior (Redl and Wineman, 1957). While economic factors have limited the availability of these therapeutic programs, the knowledge derived from them can be used in furthering understanding of developmental psychopathology. Yet it seems to us that these programs have been less successful in their expression of a clear therapeutic method for these children. The programs tried either to replace the parents (Bettelheim, 1950) or to provide the children with a different environment, based on the assumption that once children face a benevolent environment they will change their attitudes, concepts, and aggressive behavior.

THE B'NAI B'RITH WOMEN RESIDENTIAL TREATMENT CENTER IN JERUSALEM

In what follows we describe what is a unique program of residential treatment run by B'nai B'rith Women of America and located in Jerusalem, Israel. This center is devoted to intensive, psychoanalytically oriented, multimodal treatment of children with serious emotional and behavioral disorders, particularly involving conduct and aggression. The treatment is based on the primary role of interpersonal relationships in the structuring of children's internal world and the formation of increasingly mature methods of self-regulation and self-conception.

This residential treatment center (RTC) was established in 1943 and serves sixty-five children at any one time, ages 8 to 14. Another twenty youngsters, ages 14 to 18, are treated in an urban group home setting. The above-mentioned goals are achieved through a setting that is not primarily geared toward copying the real world or the family. We have constructed a system of residential treatment in which children may stay five to six years. Each child is part of a unit of twelve children who stay together for the entire treatment period, with eight staff members attached directly to each unit. This staff includes a unit coordinator, a clinical psychologist, a social worker, two child-care workers, and three teachers. This team works closely and cohesively together. The team holds several meetings per week in which the members discuss many issues with regard to the children, as well as to their own feelings (countertransference). Expressing the real feelings of frustration, failure, being undermined by the children, helplessness, and so on, is one of the major tools for being able to cope with the phenomenon of burnout. These children need constancy above all. They require staff members who are able to stay with them for the entire period of treatment (five years) and who are thus able to endure the negative feelings and emotions that emerge whenever they deal with severely emotionally disturbed children, children who hate (Redl, 1957), children who are sick of being rejected, deserted, and unwanted.

Some of the unit meetings include the entire group of children and staff, and some are held by the eight staff members together; there are also meetings of the child-care workers with their supervisors, and separate meetings of the teachers. The social worker's main role is to meet with each family separately, as the family is required to visit the residential center once a week. Furthermore, all the children receive individual psychotherapy, in addition to the therapeutic environment of the day-to-day life on campus during school and after school, that is fully geared toward the emotional well-being of the children and not primarily toward their behavior or academic achievements. Thus, though the teacher tries to teach as in any regular school, attention is focused on the emotional development of the children, on their reaction to failures and achievements, their kinds of associations, what causes them anxiety, and so on. The same applies to the daily routine: the child-care worker's aim is, on the one hand, to see to it that the children get up in the morning and dress themselves, for example; but, on the other hand, the care worker is more concerned with the children's emotional state while in the process of getting up each morning. The process of getting up in the morning is the central issue, not the specific result of this activity.

THE CLINICAL APPLICATION OF THE CONCEPT OF "POTENTIAL SPACE"

The basic assumption underlying this structure is that it contains all the factors that provide the children with the critical developmental needs of early infancy—which they never received—and I refer to what Winnicott termed "potential space." We believe that when children reach school age and are still in need of potential space, it is impossible to create it for them while they are in foster care or short-term residential treatment. Both foster care and short-term residential treatment are too similar to the reality of normal society, causing these treatment frames to be primarily directed toward adjustment issues, mainly the behavior of the children. But, as stated above, these children's main need is a well-integrated self, a personality of their own (which will also have an impact on their overall behavior, but more as a side effect). However, these statements require a short explanation of why potential space is indispensable for normal development and how this may be achieved in residential treatment.

Winnicott (1971), and later also Ogden (1985), tried to explain what takes place in normal development between an infant and its mother through the concept of potential space, which is reminiscent of a more popular concept of Winnicott's (1953)—the "transitional object." It means space of any kind, undefined, which supposedly exists between mother and child. It is the same space in which separation between them exists, while at one and the same time there also exists an almost symbiotic unity. Every glance or movement of the infant or the mother will elicit a certain response by both of them. The mother arouses something in her infant, yet there is something that the infant creates and awakens within the mother as well. In other words, it is hard to discern which of the two is the creator, the stimulator, the navigator, the initiator—the mother or the infant, or perhaps both of them together are as one inseparable unit. Within this space nonverbal communication takes place, such as the infant's crying. When potential space exists, the infant's crying acquires a unique quality of communication through common signals, which the mother senses and fully comprehends. Thus, this complicated and manifold activity of crying ceases to be just a clear-cut and sole activity. Now it encompasses the mother's presence, reactions, grimaces, and so on. The same applies to any other activity or experience the infant goes through. The nipple is not only a feeding organ but also the initiator of a whole range of tiny facial expressions and movements. The feeding activity is thus a configuration of actions, feelings, reactions, and imagination. All these phenomena take place in this special space—potential space—but only as long as the caregiver—mother—is tuned to the infant's needs, not merely its feeding needs. By these means, the infant molds itself, both as creator and initiator on the one hand, and as receiver of external signals that serve as feedback to its activities, on the other hand.

If the potential space between an infant and its mother is absent or harmed, the infant's development is deficient from the very start. For example, if the mother is totally preoccupied with herself, or uses the infant to fulfill her own needs, she does not allow this space to be created, and then certainly the infant cannot successfully develop its idiosyncratic, true self. The mother, fully engrossed in herself, will not relinquish herself; she will not funnel mental and emotional energies to the infant's needs, to its signals and cues, and certainly no unique and exclusive communication can develop between them. In this case, differentiation between the infant and its mother is formed too soon, without a transition period via a transitional object or potential space. The infant is thrown too soon into reality, so to speak, where it remains bound without being able to develop fantasy, wishes, hopes, and expectations. In different pathological situations we may find infants who are used by their mothers to fulfill their own needs, and thus are prevented from real contact with reality and are unable to form their own true and cohesive selves.

Residential treatment may perfectly fit the requirements of a potential space, namely being *neither a replica of reality nor an imaginary entity.*

The residential center may be an entity that is partly detached from the real world. What takes place at the residential center may be different from what takes place outside its gates. If in the real world there are many and varied moral and social rules, the residential center can ignore them, alter them, and act on the norm that no norms exist. When children reach the residential center, they do not receive a predetermined set of rules they are expected to obey. The norms are formed within the process of relating to a specific child, and in that sense unique norms are developed between the child and his or her caretakers. This principle means that the child (as well as the entire unit) is an active partner in creating norms, lifestyles, and even laws, which makes the entire relationship a sort of transitional object or phenomenon, in Winnicott's terms. This is similar to the infant who finds the transitional object in the real world, yet at the same time feels as if it has itself created the particular object.

I would like to use an example in illustration of the principle. A child at the RTC may plant a tree together with her child-care worker. Following the planting the child may feel like the creator of the tree. She will care for it and feel concern for it. Another child who may come later on to the RTC can pass by the tree and step on it, break it, or even destroy it. The usual reaction of a care worker may go like this: "How dare you harm the tree, a tree you have neither planted nor cared for." This kind of reaction may be correct when dealing with normal children, but not with severely emotionally disturbed children, who have no concepts of self and object. Unless one feels one's own sense of self, of creativity, of being and doing — one cannot relate to the object as an entity in its own right, as a self with an independent existence. Thus the RTC needs to find ways through which every child will be part of the creation of norms and laws, as though he hasn't come into a preordained world but rather is part of its creation, a process that unfolds each time a new child arrives.

Thus in the above example it would be much more useful therapeutically to suggest to the child a joint experience of caring for the tree and helping the tree to grow further. Once the caregiver and the child find joint ways of caring for the tree, they will create a very unique potential space and thus will be part of the growing uniqueness of the child, of his self. These joint acts between child and care worker may be very minor and may even go unnoticed by an outsider, as they include the exchange of special smiles, glances, and so on between these two persons.

INTEGRATION OF THE THERAPEUTIC USE OF POTENTIAL SPACE WITH A STRUCTURED ENVIRONMENT WITH CLEAR BEHAVIORAL LIMITS

It would be a misunderstanding to conclude that the RTC is a very permissive environment where children are allowed to do whatever they wish. The RTC has specific limits, as well as nonspecific limits. It is this combination that makes it, along with other treatment methods, so therapeutic. One has to bear in mind that we deal with schoolage children who are still partially stuck in infancy needs.

In moving away from reality, there are some external manifestations of the difference from the real world. For instance, school classes are not graded as in the real world; there are no standards of achievement expected or demanded of the child. The child and his family are not presented with a list of requirements of academic or behavioral achievements that can determine the child's "advancement," "success," or discharge from the RTC. There is a degree of vagueness and obscurity in this regard, for alongside this detachment from reality, there is, on the other hand, a substantial list of norms that exist a priori, and achievements that are expected of the child, whether they are clearly stated, just hinted at, or not said at all. It is this purposeful lack of clarity that enables potential space to exist.

While we regard this vagueness as an essential attribute for treatment, there are RTCs that act contrary to these principles. These centers have made attempts rather to increase their similarity to reality, whether by dividing the center into familylike units with multiage levels, or taking on the characteristics of a minicommunity with its own community center, local council, and so on. These attempts may have brought the residential center closer to reality, but in so doing, they have also removed it from its therapeutic nature. Those who uphold this approach of imitating reality do so out of their firm belief that a child should be returned as quickly as possible to the real and normal world, the reality that is outside the gates of the residential center, and that the child must therefore be readied for reality by confronting it in its most palpable form while still in the residential center.

Finally, we wish to describe a case that will clearly illustrate the succession of violence in the family and the residential treatment provided to this child according to our approach.

KFIR

Kfir was 7 years old when referred for residential treatment. He was hospitalized because of a severe beating by his father, on the one hand, and because of his aggressive behavior and restlessness, on the other. He was the second child born into a family that did not want him because his parents wanted a girl.

In kindergarten he had a habit of stealing food from the lunch bags of the other children. Parents complained about him to the various authorities, and there were always stories regarding his stealing, collecting cigarettes and smoking them, breaking windows of cars, setting fires in the home, and so forth. Kfir is enuretic every night. No organic cause or physiological basis has been found to justify his ravenous appetite. Both parents declare that they are frustrated and unable to deal with him, and they do not conceal the fact that there has been physical abuse, particularly on the part of the father. The father used to beat Kfir viciously, including, by the time Kfir was 3 years old, branding his hand with a white hot knife.

The father has been in prison several times for burglary, theft, and use of drugs. The mother, too, is frightened by the father's violence and has thought about divorce several times. However, one way that she has tried to prevent the father from becoming angry at her has been basically connected to Kfir: whenever she feels the father is getting angry at her, she tells him about Kfir's antics; then the father becomes vicious toward Kfir and leaves her alone.

When Kfir entered residential treatment, he had several distinctive characteristics:

1. Kfir spent much of his time speaking in grandiose terms about his home and his family, and often stated that after the next vacation period his parents would not return him to the residential

treatment center. This statement was continuously repeated with each vacation over a period of two years, without changing the text and without any deviation from the idyllic picture that Kfir painted of his family regardless of its total lack of reality. When his parents visited the center, he would complain about the beatings that he allegedly received in the center, and his parents would express their great concern during the time of their visit. Yet it was interesting that as his complaints became more and more frequent, they visited less and less.

2. Kfir exhibited extreme sadomasochistic behavior. He would frequently search through the possessions of other children and steal from them anything he could, especially sweets. He antagonized and provoked many of the children and used to hit them without provocation. Once he even stabbed a child with a food knife. He would so provoke and harass the other children that in the end he himself would be hit by them. In all of his contacts with children and with adults, his behavior appeared almost deliberately motivated by a wish to draw down on himself violence and aggression. For example, his child-care worker would report that Kfir would want to sit on his lap, but while he did so, he would try to hurt the child-care worker so severely that the child-care worker wished to stop relating to him. During these provocations, Kfir would turn to the child-care worker and say: "Come, let's see if you can break my arm." The masochistic line showed itself in other unusual behaviors, like throwing stones on himself when he received a punishment of any kind and periodically swallowing small stones.

3. Stuttering and enuresis were the other symptoms that expressed themselves during the first two years of Kfir's stay at the center.

In meetings with Kfir during their visits to the center, Kfir's parents spoke very openly about him, giving detailed descriptions of his difficulties and the unacceptable behavior that led them to feel inadequate and frustrated. They also enumerated their own cruel acts toward him, with a very emotional description of how he disgusted them and caused them to want to get away from him. While these talks seemed to give the impression that the parents were open and willing to discuss Kfir's situation, and hinted at a potential therapeutic opening, in fact their frankness extended only to the issue of Kfir and their annoyance at him. When they spoke about their other children or about themselves, it was detached from any connection to Kfir and they became even more closed and furtive. As an example, when the father was in prison, this was described by the family as his having to go on reserve army duty. It seems that Kfir fulfilled a very important purpose for both parents by being able to represent for them their own negative parts. Thus the father does not become the criminal and the one who beats Kfir, rather Kfir becomes the thief, the hitter, the one who is unable to be tolerated, the rejected one. Similarly, it is not the mother who receives the blunt end of the violence, nor is she the one who tortures and inflicts pain, rather it is Kfir who fulfills this role faithfully.

These issues appeared clearly during Kfir's psychotherapeutic hours. The following are excerpts from one psychotherapeutic session:

During this hour, Kfir decides to put on a play. He plays the role of a bank director who is giving a loan to a client. The role of the client he thrusts upon the therapist. The money is stolen from the client (the therapist) and she therefore has difficulty returning the loan that was given to her. The client calls the bank director and asks to meet with him but he is too busy. When she does come to the bank, he makes her wait a long time before receiving her and during this time embarrasses her with various denigrating comments. He demands that she immediately return the money. It then becomes clear in the play that the director of the bank is also the owner of the garage where they are stealing from the woman. She came there to have her car fixed but they always tell her that the motor is burned and they have to change many parts; they are always asking her for a lot of money. The garage owner appoints a partner — again the therapist — and Kfir, in the role of the garage owner, screams at his partner and degrades him all the time while hitting him with vicious punches. At some point later on in the story, the garage owner and his partner break into the house of the woman, who is wealthy, and steal from her the money she has in her safe. The dollhouse in the therapist's room stands in the place of the strongbox for money. While the break-in is taking place the neighbors contact the police, but the robber kills them all, the neighbors as well as the policeman. In the end he kills five billion people, all the people in the world, and all this while committing vicious and brutal acts such as cutting their necks with a saw and sticking nails in their eyes.

We can see how, during this therapy session, the boundaries are becoming more blurred. The bank director becomes the owner of the garage; he is also a robber, and then a murderer. The client (therapist) is at one instant a very poor woman, yet at the same time she is very rich, and the robber steals money from her; she has what he does not. The destruction of the person cannot be limited and requires a total annihilation—not just murder, which can transform things, but brutal acts including placing nails in the eyes. All the images of the session are based on the mechanism of splitting: there always appears one figure who has, as opposed to another who does not have, who lacks. When there is a partner, it appears that the partner is a projected part of the main figure. This projected part-object is the one who receives the vicious beatings, the one who is humiliated, despised, and rejected.

On the basis of this material, Kfir appeared to live in an undifferentiated internal world where the boundaries between himself and other persons were totally blurred. Kfir had no clear self-representation, nor did he have a clear representation of other significant persons. This fragile self-representation was based on the various roles he was required—unconsciously—to fulfill. Any description of Kfir's personality would of necessity remain incomplete, since he had not succeeded in constructing or integrating a personality of his own.

It seemed to us that our treatment of Kfir could not focus on his misbehavior alone, as had his previous institutional experience prior to his placement in residential treatment. The treatment team instead had to seek out the target of Kfir's true self. Thus, during his first phase of treatment, staff members simply stayed with him whenever he had an aggressive outburst. During such periods, he was not told anything beyond our repeated reassurances that we were there in order to protect him from his own attacks. There were occurrences where the staff had to physically restrain him, yet this was always accompanied by verbal reassurance that we wished to protect him.

But the more Kfir realized that he could count on his own inner forces, the more he realized that he was able to postpone the fulfillment of his wishes and demands and still feel strong and safe; and the more he succeeded in realizing that he was respected because of his being there—not because of his acts—the more he could express his idiosyncratic capabilities and characteristics. With this, indeed, started the second phase of his treatment—two years after being placed in our residential treatment center. Kfir then began expressing his willingness to join a soccer team outside the center and began to show signs of concern for his peers as well as being able to undertake various roles that required responsibility. The long period of contact with the same caregivers created a unique relationship different from the relationships these same caregivers created with other children of Kfir's unit.

This positive development of a boy is also dependent on the changes that take place in the relationships of his family members with him. The multimodal system of the RTC attempts to refer to the parents not only in their parental role but as human beings with needs of their own. Once the parents realize that they are regarded as persons in their own right, they begin to disentangle themselves from their complicated and harmful bonds with the child. Thus the RTC sees the parents as part of the target population.

CONCLUSION: THERAPEUTIC PRINCIPLES

All these activities are part of the uniqueness of the RTC, which is then the essence of potential space; this uniqueness is the foundation, we believe, of treating severely emotionally disturbed children. It goes without saying that this type of treatment is time-consuming and can only be accomplished over an extended period of time, for we are here referring to children upon whom calamities have fallen from their early infancy on (or even earlier, as some may claim).

Severe childhood aggression is spawned through years of children's immersion within families that, failing in their attempts to nurture them, instead stimulate their helplessness, fear, and the aggressive behaviors that become their signature. These complex origins must be met by a similarly complex therapeutic response. Long-term residential treatment provides the optimal therapeutic opportunity. Nevertheless, simple attention to specific aggressive symptoms through firm disciplinary limits is insufficient. It must be embedded within broad nurturing principles affecting a child's whole being, exemplified by the therapeutic concepts of containment and potential space.

REFERENCES

Bettelheim, B. (1950). *Love is Not Enough*. Glencoe, IL: Free Press.

Bion, W. R. (1984). *Learning from Experience*. London: Karnac.

King, R. A., and Noshpitz, J. D. (1991). *Pathways of Growth: Essentials of Child Psychiatry*, vol. 2, *Psychopathology*. New York: Wiley.

Ogden, T. H. (1985). "On Potential Space." *International Journal of Psycho-Analysis* 66:129–141.

Redl, F., and Weinman, D. (1957). *The Aggressive Child*. Glencoe, IL: Free Press.

Winnicott, D. (1953). "Transitional Objects and Transitional Phenomena: A Study of the First Not-Me Possession." *International Journal of Psycho-Analysis* 34:89–97.

_____ (1971). *Playing and Reality*. New York: Basic Books.

III

Violence in the Child's Neighborhood

Does the type of violence influence whether a child becomes symptomatic later or shows disturbed patterns of aggression when older? We particularly want to know whether it matters to the child's outcome if the violence is a natural disaster (such as an earthquake or flood), a political disaster leading to violence (the violent disintegration of his or her country), or aggressive violence between family members or others in their neighborhood. Does it affect the child's short-term outcome, long-term outcome, or both? What similarities in response by the children do we observe? Do these different types of violence require different therapeutic interventions, or is there a predictable response to any trauma that should guide professionals toward setting up a treatment protocol that will be useful for all? Who should provide the treatment, and where? Is this a matter for treatment by experts, away from the frightening scenes the children have encountered, or for caregivers closer to home in a familiar setting, physically and culturally? Have we any idea how the differences among the types of violence experienced by the child affect later outcome?

6

Community Violence and Children's Development: Collaborative Interventions

STEVEN MARANS

INTRODUCTION

Dramatic and explosive violence is a staple on the nightly news all over the world. In the United States and elsewhere many urban families, however, do not need to turn on their television set to experience violent acts. Nor can they turn them off with the touch of a dial. They hear the sound of gunfire outside their windows. They witness shootings and stabbings in their homes and streets. Both the assailants and the wounded are their relatives and neighbors. While ambulances rush the medical casualties to hospital emergency rooms, the psychological victims, children and parents who are witnesses, are left to sleep on the floors at night. They stay inside and hope that their attempts to remain physically safe will also reduce the threatening images and thoughts of violence. Too often these images and fears do not fade away, and the children, in particular, pay a high price for their exposure and forced adaptation.

For children, direct exposure to violence provokes feelings of helplessness and fear that run counter to the developing child's wish and capacity for increasing mastery of his world. Children's responses of distress may include specific symptoms of post-traumatic stress disorder — disrupted patterns of eating, sleeping,

The author gratefully acknowledges the support for this work by the Rockefeller Foundation, the Smart Family Foundation, and the B'nai B'rith Women's Organization. Parts of this work are presented in L. Leavitt and N. Fox (1993).

attention and relating, and fearfulness and flashbacks (*DSM-III-R*, 1987). Repeated, direct exposure to violence may lead to persisting patterns of adaptive but problematic behaviors and modes of functioning. The child may withdraw, appear depressed; display difficulties with school achievement and social relationships; or may assume the active role, becoming the agent of aggressive violence rather than remaining its passive victim.

Applications of principles of child and adolescent development to a variety of situations outside of the consulting room have been employed in an attempt to minimize the stress and traumatization that may interfere with children's developmental potential (Marans, 1991). Principles regarding the essential emotional needs of the child, the child's primary tie to the parent, and the potentially traumatic effects of disrupting that relationship have been applied in considering the "best interests" of children requiring hospitalization (Burlingham, 1979; Earle, 1979; Fraiberg, 1968; Freud, 1952; Furman et al., 1968; Moran, 1984; Schowalter and Lord, 1972), institutional care (Provence and Lipton, 1962; Robertson and Robertson, 1958; Spitz, 1945), and involvement in custody/placement decisions (Goldstein, 1973, 1979, 1986). In work with children and families exposed to violence, the development of a program on Child Development and Community Policing addresses another aspect of psychic trauma that occurs when what Freud referred to as the "actual danger" (Freud, 1926) is in the form of gunfire, wounding, and death. In the current collaboration developed between the Yale Child Study Center and the New Haven Department of Police Service, child analysts and analytically informed clinicians have turned to the police as the professionals who have the greatest amount of immediate and sustained contact with the children and families most directly in the line of fire.

TRENDS IN COMMUNITY VIOLENCE

While community violence in the United States by no means began in the latter part of the twentieth century, over the last several years there has been a marked increase in its occurrence. In the period between 1989 and 1990 alone, Boston experienced a 45 percent rise in rates of violence; Denver showed a 29 percent increase; Chicago, New Orleans, and Dallas each had increases of 20 percent (Surgeon General's Workshop on Violence and Public Health, 1991). During the year ending in December 1991 approximately 22, 000 people died from assaultive violence, while 2.2 million people suffered nonfatal injuries from assaultive violence (Surgeon General's Workshop on Violence and Public Health, 1992). It is estimated that homicide is the second leading cause of death among 15- to 24-year-olds in the United States. It would seem that the despair of unemployment, multigenerational poverty, and family dissolution contribute to a sense of helplessness and rage that for too many can lead them to find some relief in the power of a violent resolution of disputes.

While the statistics regarding the incidence of assaultive violence are disturbing in and of themselves, it is important to note that the potential number of children as psychological victims may far outnumber the medical casualties that reach our emergency rooms or the headlines of our newspapers. In a recent study conducted at Boston City Hospital, it is reported that one of every ten children seen in the primary care clinic there witnessed a shooting or stabbing before the age of 6 — half in the home, half on the streets. The average age of the children was 2.7 years (Taylor, 1992). In a survey of inner-city elementary school children in New Orleans, 80 percent of the sample reported witnessing violence; 60 percent had seen weapons used; 40 percent had seen a dead body (Osofsky et al., 1992). Similarly, in a study conducted in New Haven schools of sixth, eighth, and tenth graders, 40 percent reported being witness to at least one violent crime in the past year (R. Weissberg and M. Schwab-Stone, personal communication). In spite of the fact that New Haven is well endowed with mental health services for children and families, it is clear that the potential number of psychological victims of violence far outweigh the availability and responsiveness of existing models of intervention. It was out of the shared concerns about these often unnoticed psychological casualties of violence that the collaboration between the Child Study Center and the New Haven Department of Police Service emerged.

CHILD DEVELOPMENT AND COMMUNITY POLICING

The discussions that took place between the leadership of the Yale Child Study Center and the New Haven Department of Police Service occurred in the context of rising rates of violence and the recognition that previous intervention strategies on the part of police and mental health professionals were having limited impact on interrupting the trends in violence or decreasing the number of medical casualties and psychological victims of violence. The discussions also occurred in the context of a shift to community-based policing within the New Haven police service and to increasing acceptability of clinical services through schools, the home, and community resources. The Child Development-Community Policing Program is a collaborative effort to address these problems through prevention and intervention activities on the part of mental health and police professionals. The program consists of several interrelated educational and clinical components that aim at sharing knowledge between police officers and mental health professionals in the service of ameliorating some of the effects of violence on inner-city children. These components grew out of months of discussions between faculty members of the Yale Child Study Center that occurred in equal parts in conference rooms, on the streets and in squad cars, in outpatient clinics and in hospital emergency rooms, in juvenile courts and detention centers, and in substations throughout the city of New Haven. The components that were developed are:

Child Development Fellowships

Clinical fellowships were established for supervisory sergeants who spend three to four months rotating through various clinical and consultative services of the Yale Child Study Center. Under the guidance of a mentor from the clinical faculty, police fellows participate in a range of educational activities. These experiences were intended to familiarize them with developmental concepts, patterns of psychological disturbance, methods of clinical intervention, and settings for treatment and care. Their program includes participation in evaluation of children with emotional and psychiatric problems, visits with a consultation team to community schools, participation in clinical meetings with the child welfare team to discuss families in crisis, discussions with senior faculty of children and adolescents who are brought to the emergency service or are psychiatric inpatients, and attendance at seminars and other teaching activities within the Child Study Center. Participation of veteran supervisory officers in the fellowship has several aims: (1) the clinical fellowship prepares supervisory officers to provide leadership for ongoing application of developmental principles to police work by officers working under their command; (2) their years of police practice expertise has been essential in developing and implementing all other areas of the Child Development-Community Policing Program; and (3) their visibility and endorsement of the principles and practices of the program have been instrumental in gaining acceptance throughout both the police department and the department of child psychiatry within the medical school. In turn, the visibility of clinicians engaged with police officers in various domains has been equally important to the potential role of mental health clinicians as potential collaborators for police officers.

The Education of Police Officers

In New Haven, as elsewhere in the United States, the education of police officers has not specifically and prospectively prepared them for dealing with the psychological impact of violence on children, adolescents, and their families — let alone the impact on themselves. Nor has there been any particular frame of reference for considering the range of human behavior they confront and must respond to in the course of their daily work. A seminar for community-based officers was created and taught by senior officers who had completed the child development fellowship and faculty members of the Child Study Center. The twenty hours of seminars for groups no larger than fifteen participants aims at providing officers with both knowledge and a sense of personal empowerment to think about and intervene positively with children and families in a range of situations.

The major theme of the seminar is how police officers' direct experiences, enriched by knowledge from psychodynamic theories of development, can lead to useful understanding of the phenomenology of human behavior. Topics include the phases of child development and how these are shaped by different types of experiences within the family and community; social structures that influence individuals' sense of themselves, their families, and social groups; sources of security for individuals, types of dangers, traumas, and stress experienced; varying patterns of coping; and how to communicate with and understand children and youth at different times, including when they are witnesses to and victims of violence and other trauma. The seminars are interactive and informal and employ both individual cases and specific scenarios from police experience as starting points for teaching about general principles of development and psychological functioning. An essential ingredient to officers' participation in these discussions is the notion and experience that when officers have a broader frame of reference for understanding human behavior, their options for safer, more creative, and more effective interventions are expanded.

Consultation Service

When an officer comes into contact with a child or youth in danger or distress, he or she must make an immediate decision about whether to intervene and what is in the child's best interests. At times, the path of intervention is clearly mandated, as when a child is thought to be the victim of abuse or neglect and the state child welfare agency must be notified. At other times the critical nature of a medical condition, for example, following an assault or a suicide attempt, dictates the involvement of emergency medical services. However, officers are most often faced with more ambiguous situations, situations in which there is no clearly mandated or available service. An officer who finds children who have been witnesses to an accident or assault, who has a teenager confide in him about being worried about gang involvements, or who observes a child becoming a chronic truant may have opportunities for intervention broader than those usually seen as within the province of police work. It is at the officer's discretion how to proceed. As police officers work more closely with communities, these situations occur with greater frequency. Where might an officer turn for discussion, guidance, and an immediate clinical response? This is especially critical when the officer is confronted by a child who is in great distress or who has quietly withdrawn at the scene of horrific violence.

The consultation service allows police officers to make referrals and to have clinicians respond to their immediate needs. Child Development-Community Policing (CD-CP) clinicians and senior police officers are on call twenty-four hours a day to discuss children and youth with police officers. Many consultations lead to a disposition to an appropriate service agency, for example, the state child protection agency, an appointment at the Child Study Center or other child guidance services within the community, or engagement with the mental health team within the child's school. However, at other times a direct clinical response is indicated due to the urgency of the situation or because of our increased awareness that an immediate response to the child and family at the scene of a violent event can, in fact, set the stage for the clinician's closer understanding of the magnitude of the experience and may enhance the potential for a therapeutic contact being made. At these times CD-CP clinicians and officers can respond immediately and see children and their families in the home, at the Child Study Center, or in the neighborhood substation or police headquarters.

Case Conference

During and after their involvement in the clinical fellowship, police officers and faculty within the Child Study Center meet on a weekly basis to discuss difficult and perplexing cases that arise from our direct experiences through the consultation service. The case discussions emphasize the importance of trying to understand the inner experience and the meaning of events to children, adolescents, and their families, as well as the challenges and difficulties in the path of the service providers. These discussions address the ways in which psychological understanding can guide both police and clinical work. A case conference also offers the clinical fellows and Child Study faculty an opportunity to continue and elaborate their working relationships with one another. Increasingly, as these meetings are held in the substations around the city of New Haven, more and more officers are able to participate in these meetings as a way of continuing their engagement in discussions that are often similar to ones that they may have experienced in their ten-week seminars.

During the first year and a half of operation, the program has trained 150 officers in the seminars on child and adolescent development; 15 supervisory officers, including the assistant chief of police, have participated in the clinical fellowship; and approximately 200 children have been seen through the consultation service.

CHILDREN'S RESPONSES TO VIOLENCE

The children we have seen have ranged in age from 2 to 17 years. Initial contact has occurred from within minutes of a violent event to several days after and has included children's exposure to shootings, stabbings, beatings, and in one situation, the drowning death of a peer. The traumatic situation may still be described as one in which the individual has experienced feelings of helplessness in the face of a danger whose magnitude outweighs the "subject's estimation of his own strength" (Freud, 1926, p. 166). The children we have seen through the consultation service have responded to the violence they have witnessed with a variety of defensive activities that may best be seen as attempts to regain a semblance of control, strength, power, and predictability; to gain distance from, and better prepare for the images and feelings associated with danger and fear.

Similar to the findings of other investigators (Pynoos et al., 1987; Pynoos and Nader 1989; Terr, 1991) our observations suggest that the degree of a child's disturbance or traumatization is determined by an interplay of factors within the child and between the child and his or her surroundings:

- characteristics of the violence itself — that is, the child's relationship to the perpetrator and victim, proximity to the incident, response of the caregivers to the incident.
- the developmental phase of the child who is exposed — that is, the status of emotional and cognitive resources available for mediating anxiety associated with objective and fantasized dangers.
- the familial and community context of the violent incident — that is, was the incident isolated and unusual, or part of a chronic pattern of daily life.
- recognition of and sustained responses to the possible effects of the child's exposure to violence by family members, school personnel, and community institutions.

In addition, while there is tremendous variation among children seen by consultation service clinicians and police officers, some common observations can be reported. These include: (1) disbelief and denial of the outcome or even the occurrence of the violent event; (2) intense longing for the presence of and concern about the safety of primary caregivers (especially among children under age 7); (3) revival of and much talk about previous losses, injuries, fights, and other episodes of violence; (4) repetitive retelling of the events with ideas that might have altered the real outcome of the episode, described by Pynoos as "intervention strategies" (R. Pynoos, personal communication); (5) attribution of blame to those not directly involved in the violence; or alternatively (6) reveling in the excitement of the action of the violence with talk of the weapons used, who got "capped," "smoked," or "aired."

While our findings are preliminary, it would appear that two groups of children are most vulnerable to longer term presentation of affective, attentional, and behavioral difficulties in the wake of their exposure to episodes of violence. Not surprisingly, one group includes children whose development has already appeared compromised and whose limited capacity for mediating anxiety led to a range of symptoms prior to witnessing a violent event. The second group of children includes those whose initial responses are quiet and unobtrusive to the adult caregivers or whose gross symptomatology is not seen by caregivers as causally linked to the child's exposure to a disturbing scene of violence. When the child is unable to understand, let alone directly verbalize his or her experience of trauma, adults are often unable to listen to or interpret the child's action or symptomatic language that communicates distress. Additionally, adults may be overwhelmed by the child's feelings of helplessness and fear, so similar to those that accompany their own experiences of violent episodes. Their own inability to listen and to attend to their child's needs may be a natural consequence of their own attempts at restitution and self-protection and feelings of vulnerability—the wish to push away upsetting images and feelings is especially powerful when the events that evoke them are so dangerous and real.

These phenomena have a special bearing on mental health care providers and police officers as well. By personal disposition and training, each is called upon to treat and cure the ills of patients or to "protect and serve" citizens to the best of their personal abilities and the community's resources. In cases involving children who have witnessed incidents of violence, however, the professionals who respond to them are not immune to the horrors that the children have experienced themselves. The urge to act, to make things better quickly for patients or the youngest citizens served, may be an attempt to guard against the discomfort and feelings of helplessness experienced by the professionals, while interfering with the most significant initial intervention that the professionals have to offer—to listen and to attend.

COLLABORATIVE INTERVENTIONS: A FAMILY WITNESSES MURDER

Through the collaboration between police officers and clinicians, the Child Development-Community Policing Program has led to innovative methods for clinical intervention in relation to children who have been victims of violence. Their cases reveal the depth of traumatization to which inner-city children are exposed and the ways in which police and mental health professionals complement each other in trying to respond effectively.

Mr. and Ms. Rodriguez live in a public housing project in New Haven with their 2½- and 10-year-old sons, Manuel and George. Both Isabel and Martin Rodriguez are unemployed and live on AFDC (Aid to Families with Dependent Children) payments they receive from the state. On a Saturday morning in January, Martin's brother Julio raced into the apartment and claimed that four men with guns were chasing him. Ms. Rodriguez called the police and waited for them to arrive as the men attempted to batter down the apartment door. Julio tried to secure the door by leaning against it and pleaded with the men to let him come outside and talk because there were children inside. As Ms. Rodriguez phoned the police again, Julio was shot through the door; he fell into the living room, bleeding profusely from a bullet wound to the chest. The shooter then battered the door down, and walked around the apartment pointing his gun at everyone, including the children who now stood over the body of their uncle. After ripping the phone off the wall, the assailant backed out of the room with his gun trained on Ms. Rodriguez. The police and an ambulance arrived moments later. The shooter and his three accomplices were arrested; Julio died en route to the hospital.

On the day of the shooting two New Haven police sergeants involved in the investigation referred the Rodriguez family to the consultation service. Both officers were part of the Child Study Center training program. While the family initially declined immediate contact with a clinician, they were eager to have the officers' beeper numbers and in the following days made frequent calls describing fears of further shootings, as well as multiple symptoms that both children and adults were experiencing. The officers were in daily contact with the psychiatric social worker assigned to the case, who advised them to gently press the idea of meeting with her. Six days after the shooting, Mr. Rodriguez left the home, claiming that he was unable to remain in the apartment where his brother had been killed. At this point Ms. Rodriguez accepted the referral for services from the Child Study Center. Because of transportation problems, the family was initially seen in their home.

Ms. Rodriguez and her two sons were having difficulty falling asleep at night and were waking frequently during the night. Two-year-old Manuel was very clingy with his mother, demanded to be held and carried, hunted around the apartment for his father, and asked frequently where his father was. Ms. Rodriguez described Manuel as having previously been an active and independent child. She reported some success in soothing him by giving him a bottle, from which he had previously been weaned. Ten-year-old George was having nightmares, waking frequently, checking that doors and windows were locked, and insisted on sleeping in his mother's bed. George also reported that he was nervous and scared all the time, couldn't stop thinking about the shooting, worried that the shooter would come back, and felt afraid to be outside alone. This meant that he could not walk the few blocks to his aunt's house. Ms. Rodriguez reported sleeplessness, nervousness and jitteriness, and preoccupation with thoughts about the shooting and worries that she and her children were not safe. During the interview she was unable to sit still and was frequently tearful. Ms. Rodriguez had seen her primary physician, who had given her a prescription for a mild sedative to be taken at bedtime, but she had been afraid to take the medication because it might make her sleep so deeply that she would not be able to rouse herself in case of another emergency.

The family was seen on four occasions in their home. Most of the meetings took place with all three family members present because there was little private space in the apartment. During some of the meetings Manuel was either sleeping or was willing to play by himself in another room. It was apparent that Ms. Rodriguez and George had talked a lot about the incident and neither seemed surprised by anything the other said, although they did disagree about some details of the events.

The first meeting focused primarily on a description of the traumatic events and the witnesses' reactions. Both Ms. Rodriguez and George were eager to describe what had happened and to show the clinician where all the participants had been and the damage that remained in the apartment. In Ms. Rodriguez's

account, the most prominent details concerned her own helplessness and the helplessness of those around her. She repeatedly told
of having been on the telephone trying to get help when the shot
came through the door, and also focused on Julio's ineffective
plea to the shooter not to come into the apartment where there
were children. Ms. Rodriguez also reported feeling afraid in her
apartment but unable to go anywhere else. George's account of the
shooting focused more on the gruesomeness of the scene. He was
preoccupied with the images of blood on the floor, blood on his
own clothing, and having been touched by Julio as he fell into the
living room. George pointed out what was left of the bloodstain
on the rug and described feeling afraid to walk on the rug,
especially on or near the stain. George was also preoccupied with
concrete issues of physical security in the apartment, for example,
whether the spackle patch of the bullet hole in the door might fall
out. During the first meeting the clinician responded by agreeing
that the events described had really been horrible and overwhelm-
ing, and explained that the reactions the family described were
expectable reactions to a traumatic experience. The clinician
discussed with Ms. Rodriguez the boys' experience of losing their
father at the same time as witnessing the shooting and urged her to
make some arrangement for them to have contact with their
father.

In subsequent meetings in the home, Ms. Rodriguez was agitated but more angry than she had been initially. Her anger was
directed at the landlord, who had not made needed repairs in the
apartment and threatened to charge her for the cost of repairing
the battered door, and also at Mr. Rodriguez, who had not called
her on Christmas, had not arranged to see Manuel, and had
chosen to stay with his father rather than her. She was also
reexamining his actions during the shooting, and felt enraged that
he had not provided any protection or assistance to her or the
children but had hidden himself in the bedroom.

During the later home visits George talked about his vengeful
fantasies about what should happen to the shooter, his continuing
fears about his own safety, his wish to live in an apartment with a
security system, and his fantasies about dangerous and magical
properties of the bloodstained rug (e.g., to make a battery-
powered toy operate without batteries). The clinician encouraged
both George and Ms. Rodriguez to differentiate their fantasies of
danger and magic from what they knew was real and recom-

mended to Ms. Rodriguez that she come to the outpatient clinic with her children so they could obtain longer-term help coping with this crisis than could be provided in their home.

In the course of this initial evaluation period, George was friendly, verbal, and engaging as he described his sleep difficulties; anxious, intrusive thoughts about his safety; and restricted activities that followed the shooting. He was pleased to be offered the chance for further discussions in order to feel better and had already felt some relief from his talks with the evaluating clinician. While it appeared that George was very attached to his mother and sought comfort from her when he was scared, he was also burdened by her obvious distress and made frequent efforts to comfort her, especially when she cried.

Ms. Rodriguez herself was extremely anxious and sought constant contact and reassurance from the police and the clinician regarding her family's safety and emotional and physical needs. In spite of "on-call" availability of both, Ms. Rodriguez was overwhelmed. She saw herself as passive, dependent, and helpless. She was unable to make realistic efforts to secure new housing for her family and unwilling to take prescribed medication that would help diminish her level of immobilizing anxiety. Reassuring her about the safety of the medication, the clinician capitalized on Ms. Rodriguez' genuine concerns about her children and their need for her optimal stability to help them with the distressing events. In addition, the combined efforts of the clinician and community police officer involved in the case eventually guided her to the appropriate public housing authorities for discussions about a possible change of neighborhoods.

During the initial contact with the Rodriguez family it became apparent that George's acute, post-traumatic symptoms were predated by long-standing social and academic difficulties that had never been evaluated or treated. While 2-year-old Manuel was able to once again give up his bottle and return to his previous good level of functioning on his father's return home, more extensive treatment for George and his mother was indicated. Both were referred to the outpatient clinic of the Child Study Center for individual and family psychotherapy. Transportation was arranged by the CD/CP clinician and the community-based police officer who later engaged George in an after-school program sponsored by the police. As the post-traumatic stress symptoms abated for both George and Ms. Rodriguez, the emphasis of the clinical work shifted from the crisis that followed the shooting to long-standing difficulties with self-esteem, mutual dependence, and constriction of more age-appropriate autonomous functioning.

DISCUSSION

As the rate of violence within our inner cities has climbed, so has the number of children who are its physical casualties and psychological victims. Often the families most affected by community violence have limited access to mental health services or are unable to take advantage of those that exist. Feelings of hopelessness conspire with the burdens of transportation and the weariness of social service institutions to limit utilization of existing clinical services. Moreover, it is not easy for adult caregivers to attend, listen, and understand a child's efforts at recovering from trauma when the need to push away their own experience of fear, helplessness, and discomfort in the face of violence is so great. When attention is not paid, when there are no interventions for the psychological victims of violence, they run the risk of never fully recovering; they continue to pay a high price for their exposure. They may be unable to concentrate and learn, unable to feel safe in play, and may eventually find some degree of safety and power only as the agent of violence, rather than as its victim.

In the collaborative effort between mental health and police professionals developed in New Haven, the Child Development-Community Policing Program is broadening the potential sites for providing informed and consistent attention to children at greatest risk for developmental difficulties, symptoms, and self-destructive responses that might result if their exposure to community violence goes unnoticed and unattended.

REFERENCES

American Psychiatric Association. (1987). *Diagnostic and Statistical Manual of Mental Disorders*. 3rd ed., revised. Washington, D.C.: American Psychiatric Association.

Burlingham, D. (1979). "To be Blind in a Sighted World." *Psychoanalytic Study of the Child* 34:5–30.

Earle, E. (1979). "The psychological Effects of Mutilating Surgery." *Psychoanalytic Study of the Child* 34:527–546.

Fraiberg, S. (1968). *Insights from the Blind*. New York: Basic Books.

Freud, A. (1952). "The Role of Bodily Illness in the Mental Life of Children." *Psychoanalytic Study of the Child* 7:69–81.

Freud, S. (1926). "Inhibitions, Symptoms, and Anxiety." *Standard Edition* 20:77–174.

Furman, E., Solnit, A., Lang, J., et al. (1968). "Symposium: Child Analysis and Pediatrics." *International Journal of Psychoanalysis* 49:276.

Goldstein, J., Freud, A., Solnit, A. (1973). *Beyond the Best Interests of the Child*. New York: Free Press.

_____ (1979). *Before the Best Interests of the Child*. New York: Free Press.

_____ (1986). *In the Best Interests of the Child*. New York: Free Press.

Marans, S., and Cohen, D. (1991). "Child Psychoanalytic Theories of Development." In *Child and Adolescent Psychiatry: A Comprehensive Textbook*, ed. M. Lewis. Baltimore: Williams & Wilkins.

_____ (1993) "Children and Inner-City Violence: Strategies for Intervention." In *The Psychological Effects of War and Violence on Children*, ed. L. Leavitt and N. Fox, pp. 218–301. Hillsdale, NJ: Lawrence Erlbaum.

Moran, G. (1984). "Psychoanalytic Treatment of Diabetic Children." *Psychoanalytic Study of the Child* 39:407–447.

Osofsky, J., Wewer, S., Hann, D., and Fick, A. (1992). Cited in *Can They Feel Safe Again? The Impact of Community Violence on Infants, Toddlers, Their Parents and Practitioners: Zero to Three*. Arlington, Va.: National Center for Clinical Infant Programs.

Provence, S., and Lipton, R. (1962). *Infants in Institutions*. New York: International Universities Press.

Pynoos, R., Frederick, C., Nader, K., et al. (1987). "Life Threat and Posttraumatic Stress in School-Aged Children." *Archives of General Psychiatry* 44:1057–1063.

Pynoos, R., and Nader, K. (1989). "Children's Memory and Proximity to Violence." *Journal of the American Academy of Child and Adolescent Psychiatry* 28, no. 2:236–241.

Robertson, J., and Robertson, J. (1958). *Young Children in Hospital*. New York: Basic Books.

Schowalter, J., and Lord, J. (1972). "On the Writings of Adolescents in a General Hospital Ward." *Psychoanalytic Study of the Child* 27:181–200. New Haven: Yale University Press.

Spitz, R. (1945). "Hospitalism: An Inquiry into the Genesis of Psychiatric Conditions in Childhood." *Psychoanalytic Study of the Child* 1:53–74.

Surgeon General's Workshop on Violence and Public Health. (1991).

Violence in America: A Public Health Approach, ed. M. Rosenberg and M. Fenley. Oxford: Oxford University Press.

Taylor, L., Zuckerman, B., Harik, V., and Groves, B. (1992). "Exposure to Violence among Inner City Parents and Young Children." *American Journal of Diseases of Children* 146:487–494.

Terr, L. (1991). "Childhood Traumas: An Outline and Overview." *American Journal of Psychiatry* 148:10–20.

7

Earthquake in Armenia: Establishment of a Psychological Care Center

MARIE ROSE MORO

Medical activities in emergency situations such as natural catastrophes, war, or refugee camps are now common practice. They have been standardized and evaluated. The same cannot be said about psychological triage and treatment activities. Are these circumstances of medical emergencies also psychological emergencies? If so, how do we plan, implement, and evaluate the effectiveness of psychological interventions? The earthquake in Armenia in 1988 encourages us to answer such questions and to establish a new framework for intervention adapted to the seriousness of the situation and to the political, geographical, cultural, and social context. This pioneering experience was forced on us by the intensity of the psychological distress experienced in the field, especially among children.

THE SITUATION AND THE PROBLEMS ENCOUNTERED

The Earthquake

On 7 December 1988 the most deadly earthquake of the past ten years took place in Armenia. In a population of 3.3 million in Soviet Armenia, an estimated 25,000 to 100,000 people died. Another 15,000 people wounded and 500,000 to 700,000 left homeless brings the total of those affected to close to 60 percent of the population living in the region of the earthquake.

Léninakan was 75 percent destroyed. Spitak and Nalband were taken off the map. Kirovakan and Stepanavan were very badly damaged, as were at least fifty villages in this area of northern Armenia. Families were broken up, sometimes displaced, and always torn apart. The heavy losses appear to have been due as much to the inadequacy of structures built in a region known to be at risk as to the disorganization of initial local rescue attempts.

Clinical Problems Encountered

Children were severely affected either directly (deaths, wounds) or indirectly by the death of a parent or a relative, and by the disorganization of the family and of the school. From the beginning of humanitarian activities, reports of physicians stressed the appearance of numerous psychological problems among the affected population, especially among children, who were designated as an overwhelmingly affected group. A study by the Médecins du Monde reported that 70 percent of children within the destroyed region had serious signs of trauma. Initial reports by psychologists and psychiatrists in the field were sent by the Médecins Sans Frontières (MSF), and later our own observations confirmed these first impressions. Both Médecins du Monde and MSF are international humanitarian organizations.

Children presented massive and often varied pathology. The most frequent problems are summarized in table 7–1 and detailed below.

Infants and toddlers under 3 years of age

- Sudden appearance of functional symptoms for which no organic cause was identified: sleep problems, anorexia, vomiting, dermatological lesions
- Babies are inhibited and sad, with disturbances of tone and behavior
- Frequent difficulties in mother–infant relations (global dysfunction or feeding and sleeping problems)

Children and adolescents from 3 to 18 years

- Behavioral problems as frequent at school as at home; a problem with mourning often the cause

Table 7-1 *Frequency of Symptoms*

Symptoms	Frequency (in %)
Behavior problems	57.1
Fears and phobias	48.3
Sleeping problems	34.1
Anxiety and depression	22.1
Sphincter problems	15.1
Somatic problems	10.1
Language, stuttering, and tic problems	9.8
Mother–child interaction problems	7.3
Psychomotor problems	5
Eating disorders	4.7
Illusions and pseudo-hallucinations	1.9

Note: the total is greater than 100 percent, as the children could present many associated symptoms.
Source: EPIINFO and Terrain.

- Varied phobias, appearing suddenly: school phobias, social phobias, intense and multiple fears (fear of dogs, "spirits," "Turks," "Russians")
- Sleeping problems (difficulties falling sleep, anxiety dreams, anxious awakenings) almost systematic among affected children but are in general transitory; for some, however, these problems are lasting
- Diffuse, intrusive anxiety frequently associated with depressive symptoms, common among adolescents
- Toileting problems often reactivated from early childhood and linked to other symptoms
- Frequent functional somatic problems, such as abdominal pains without an identifiable organic cause, migraine pain
- Obvious stuttering, language problems, or severe multiple tics
- Psychomotor problems range from a newly appearing clumsiness to an incapacity to carry out tasks the child was able to accomplish previously
- Eating disorders, most often anorexia or highly rigid eating habits, very upsetting to parents suffering serious food shortages
- Acute learning difficulties at school, and occasional serious memory problems
- The phenomena of illusions and "pseudo-hallucinations" dis-

concerted the first French teams. Children saw "spirits" and supernatural figures, and they heard the voices of the dead and supernatural beings . . .

- The life of the child is sometimes disturbed by serious aggressive behavior, destructive urges, or severe hyperactivity.
- Inhibition, passivity, loss of self-confidence . . . are often mentioned by the parents, even when these symptoms do not attract attention until much later.

The most urgent clinical questions concerned how to treat the consequences of the trauma: fear, mourning, loss, and anxiety about death among children, some of whom were wandering the streets (others were left entire days, without anything to do, next to their sad parents, who were discouraged and depressed to have lost a parent or work or a home).

Technical Problems Encountered

First Attempts and the Need for Innovation

Confronted with this picture of psychological distress, the first reaction of the humanitarian organizations was to send Western psychiatrists and psychologists to the site to attempt to treat the children. Prompt psychological interventions in the field rapidly proved inadequate and ineffective.

The Armenians then appealed to MSF to come up with a system to address the long-term care of the children and families suffering from the earthquake. But what type of plan could be devised in this context? At this point I was solicited by the MSF to set up a treatment facility adapted to the seriousness of the situation and to the specific needs of the Armenian population. We had no precedent to rely on, and therefore had to design and introduce our own plan of action.

My tasks, as technical director for this mission, were several: (1) to assess the psychological needs of the population; (2) to assess current and potential Armenian resources at administrative and professional levels; (3) to set up a structure adapted to the situation; (4) to supervise the functioning of the center and to evaluate the effectiveness of the program.

In order to accomplish this, I made roughly ten trips to Armenia from October 1989 through July 1992. These trips enabled me to establish fruitful exchanges on a continuing basis with Armenian families and professionals (psychologists, educators, doctors, teachers, anthropologists, etc.). I also met several university professors responsible for the training of psychologists, educators, and psychiatrists in Armenia. Finally, I led negotiations with Armenian authorities in Erevan and in Léninakan (ministry of health, ministry of education, political officials) as well as with Soviet authorities in Moscow (Since Armenia was not independent of the former USSR at the time).

The assessment of the available local resources rapidly revealed multiple technical limitations and forced us to innovate; we were happy to use our method of working in France, adapting it to the circumstances of the earthquake.

Difficulties in Dealing with Armenian Professionals

Armenia had fully trained psychiatrists and psychologists. But the psychiatrists largely dispensed psychotropic medications and had little training or apparent interest in clinical work; and the psychologists' training focused primarily on genetic and educational approaches. However, it was among the psychologists that we found the greatest number of professionals interested in being clinically trained. We thus abandoned any idea of working with the psychiatrists; the clinicians we trained were all psychologists. The training for school teachers emphasized orderliness and educational methods.

Paradoxically, at the same time I noted a fascination with psychoanalysis among the Armenian professionals. For a long time psychoanalytic literature had circulated in secret in English translations, as well as in Russian translations that were more or less reliable. Most of the professionals who had access to these texts had a "devitalized" concept of psychoanalysis because it had no link to a personal psychoanalytic experience or to clinical practice; it was an abstract psychoanalysis. My training is as a psychoanalyst, so I knew that one cannot train psychoanalysts hastily and that to give them any such illusion would be dishonest. We had to begin modestly by training clinicians locally.

Another misconception was repeated to me in the field as well as to the local ministries: "The French, the Americans . . . are capable of treating everything, but we don't know anything . . .; do it for us." But at the same time, I often heard from the same people, "You cannot understand the Armenian mentality, our ways of doing things, our intimate thoughts."

Now the importance of social and cultural symbols, coming into play as much in the expression of the psychological suffering as in the manner of thinking about it and soothing it, could not be ignored. During the first consultations and meetings we could see the reality of the cultural structure in the way people were relating, ways of representing the nature of children, relations between the generations, and the interpretations of dreams; we were also able to perceive a wealth of rituals (rituals of bereavement, of protection, etc.) and the culture's way of managing bereavement.

The complexity of these symbols implied the need for implementing a system in which the Armenians would play a predominant role. What was needed was a sufficiently flexible structure that left room for Armenian growth and creativity. In this way, the plan did not become an artificial veneer of a system whose later effectiveness risked being compromised by its foreignness, though setting up such a structure was tempting at first.

How to Act?

In order to manage these contradictions, we decided on a plan of action-training (doing things *with* them), rather than the choice of substitution (doing things *instead* of them) or affiliation (affiliating them to a psychoanalytic school, for example). We thought of this action-training plan as true cobuilding between the Armenians and ourselves.

It was therefore necessary to train the Armenians in a local clinic, a clinic without instruments (Chiland, 1983, p. 11). Our goal was to welcome the children who had suffered from the earthquake, to treat them, and to take this opportunity to train local teams who would then be able to accomplish this work on their own. Given the urgency and the lack of clinical training we chose a very pragmatic solution. The work would be done by the Armenians themselves, under the supervision and training of the French — a kind of on-the-job training, day to day, according to the care needed.

Taking into account all of these clinical and technical difficulties, we defined the operating principles of a permanent care center associating clinicians and educators, French and Armenians, care and training. Within this context, these principles had to be as economical and practical as possible; that is, starting with local possibilities, whatever their advantages and limitations.

WORKING METHODS FOR RESPONDING TO PROBLEMS ENCOUNTERED

The Team

The Armenian team is composed, on average, of six educators, four psychologists, two receptionists, and interpreters who translate methodically between French and Armenian. The team was formed progressively and underwent modification over time. In total, six psychologists and about ten educators were trained. At the beginning, we started with one psychologist, and others came to work with us right away once they recognized the efficacy of the work being done.

The Armenian team was supervised by an educator, a French clinical psychologist, a coordinator, and an MSF administrator, though if needed, two psychologists or two educators participated. Three MSF teams succeeded one another, each staying about six months.

Before the opening of the center, some psychologists and educators had already taken part as observers at consultations conducted by the French clinicians. Then several days of theoretical training centered on clinical approaches, the first consultation with a child and his family, and establishment of the role of the clinician took place. The training ultimately was associated with the specific needs of the child and the management of children's groups. This training was provided for the entire team.

The center began receiving children on 1 December 1989.

Consultations and Group Activities

The center comprises a consulting room for psychologists and a room for group therapy activities led by educators. The combination of consultations and group activities was imperative given the intensity of the clinical picture of the children and the necessity to diversify therapeutic tools in order to respond to changing situations. The group activities are numerous and age adapted (local games, fairy tales, theater, songs, rhymes, sports activities, etc.). They are all linked to ways of doing things and to traditional ways of playing in Armenia (explained by the local team of psychologists, educators, elementary school teachers, teams of nursery and kindergarten teachers, as well as anthropologists). One of the essential principles is, therefore, the use of local ways of doing things.

No medication is used in the center. All consultations and group activities are directly carried out by Armenian psychologists and educators accompanied by a small French team.

Initial Method of Carrying Out an Assessment

The first consultation is with the children and their families. The consultation is carried out by an Armenian psychologist and is conducted in Armenian. A French psychologist and his or her interpreter are nearby. Both of them stay in the background and do not directly take part in the consultation. The interpreter is also trained in clinical work and translates, word by word, the dialogue between the patient and the psychologist. The Armenian psychologist inserts regular pauses so that the translation can be given. In this way, the interpretation is directly integrated into the consultation.

Naturally, the presence of two active observers in the consultation introduces numerous biases into the development of the discussion. However, far from considering them as obstacles, we think of them as elements deliberately set into the framework. In this way, we rapidly noticed that for the patients, the act of translation is perceived as a possibility of passing from one universe to another, an act they comment on and use. In the same way, the presence of several professionals to welcome them is perceived as the reconstruction of a group who would give them a lift like the group that supports the individual in traditional Armenian society. The importance of belonging to the group among Armenians has been documented (Kasbarian-Bricout, 1990).

The French psychologist is introduced to the family and they must agree to his or her presence. The family is told that it is the Armenian psychologist who will direct the consultation. The clinical assessment done by the Armenian psychologist is conceptualized in the following manner: (1) establish a relationship with the child and her family; (2) describe the child's symptoms and place them in the framework of her history; (3) explore the ideas of the family concerning the nature of the child, her suffering, and so on; (4) reconstruct potentially traumatic events that have affected the life of the child and her family; (5) allow the child to tell about the experience of the earthquake, losses in her family, and among close relatives; (6) assess the functioning of the family; (7) identify methods for rebuilding already utilized by the family (reorganization of the family life, rituals of mourning, etc.).

The assessment is performed in three sessions, one session with the whole family, another session with the child alone, and a third session with the family again. With the child alone, the Armenian clinician uses the elements that classically permit the establishment of a relationship, the exploration of worries, the imaginary and fantasy life of the child: drawings, squiggles (Winnicott, 1971), psychodrama, and, generally speaking, any play that enables the child to engage in creative activity. The choice depends on the age of the child and preferences of the child and the clinician. The third session consists of a recapitulation of what has been understood by the clinician and permits a negotiation with the family concerning further methods for follow-up care.

After one or, usually, two consultations, the clinician gives instructions and describes the methods for caring for the patient. In the beginning, in fact, the instructions are proposed following the second consultation, which makes it possible to accomplish a thorough analysis of the work between the two meetings. Each consultation lasts approximately one hour and is followed by explanation and supervision of the same length of time. The two psychologists and the interpreter participate in this supervisory session. It is structured around the following axes: (1) synthesis of the information received and identification of the parts that are missing; (2) analysis of the difficulties experienced in establishing a relationship with the family or the child; (3) analysis of difficulties the Armenian clinician might have when assessing family and individual functioning; (4) analysis of interventions by the Armenian clinicians and of the countertransference of the Armenian and French clinicians—this phase is very important within the framework of the training of the Armenian professionals, and gave us the most trouble in the beginning; (5) discussion concerning the proposed follow-up.

Criteria for Admission into the Center

Admission criteria were defined based on the potential for accommodating children, for providing care, and for achieving the objectives of the center: (1) age below 18 years; (2) children showing symptoms that appeared or became much more severe in the weeks following the earthquake. We excluded nonpsychiatric pediatric pathologies (brain trauma, neurological pathologies, and somatic ailments), organic psychiatric pathologies (degenerative illnesses, childhood psychoses, chronic epilepsies), and chronic psychological pathologies requiring immediate long-term therapy (preexisting, nonreactive symptoms). Children presenting with these pathologies were directed to Léninakan.

All the children followed in the center presented symptoms linked, at least in part, to the earthquake. Sometimes what was involved is an aggravation of minor troubles that existed prior to the earthquake. Most of the symptoms appeared in the weeks following the earthquake, but some appeared several months later, following a precipitating event such as the birth of a sibling, the death of a relative, a separation—that is, as aftereffects. We are still within the period of reactive pathology related to the earthquake, the specific area of our intervention.

The concept *reactive* is the major criterion for admission. This criterion has been retained for practical reasons: to deal rapidly with the most urgent matters, to prevent aggravation of situations that are a priori rapidly soluble, to take into account the utilization of the Armenian clinicians.

Indications

Following a clinical assessment, the Armenian psychologist can propose several options for care. He or she can combine several options, either simultaneously or consecutively, depending on developments. The therapeutic strategy must first adapt itself to the uniqueness of the situation. The various modalities were introduced over time at the center.

Individual Consultations

The child is followed during regular meetings in the course of which the clinician explores with him his fears, his concerns, his internal conflicts. The family is generally seen at the beginning of the consultation.

Family Consultations

The child and his family are followed during regular meetings in the course of which the clinician explores and attempts to modify the difficulties in communication among the different members of the family and the conflicts between them. These meetings are proposed when the child's symptoms are recognized as being directly linked to a family problem.

Individual or Group Relaxation Sessions

These activities take place under the technical supervision of the French psychologist.

Group Therapy Activities

The purpose is to establish groups of five to six children, matched by age. Based on intervention activities, groups offer a framework that allows establishing a relationship with the children, reviving vital processes: playing, thinking, imagining, telling stories. These groups also facilitate interactions between peers. Children come once a week.

In the activities center, the work is basically performed by the teachers. Frequent meetings allow joint work with the psychologists. The activity group is headed by one or two Armenian educators. The meeting is prepared for one hour with a French educator. Then, in the course of the activity group meeting, the visiting educator is present on the same terms as those encountered by the psychologist, but translation takes place simultaneously in a low voice. The meeting lasts two hours and is followed by an analysis of one hour, bringing together the Armenian educator, the French educator, and the interpreter.

The objectives of this training supervision are as follows: (1) to assess the functioning of the group; (2) to assess difficulties in making the group function and in establishing a relationship with each child; (3) to assess difficulties in implementing the technical educational elements (play, activity, etc.); (4) to assess the countertransference and the images that the French educators and Armenian educators have in relation to the children; (5) to assess the children's development.

Within this group of activities, we must distinguish two specific groups taken care of by a psychologist and a teacher simultaneously: the mother–child group and the adolescent group.

The mother–child group (composed of two to three
mother–baby dyads)

The children are under three years. However, children even a little older, who present separation problems, are also included in these mother–child groups. During the first phase, the mothers meet with the Armenian psychologist in a room and talk about their difficulties, about their worries concerning the child, as well as the mothers' own worries. A door, always open, leads to a second room where the children are gathered around a teacher. Activities are provided to them according to their age. They can also stay with their mothers or go back and forth. The second phase gathers everybody together.

The adolescent group (composed of four to five adolescents
between 14 and 18 years of age)

Expressive activities are conducted in the adolescent language that is used in their real-life activities.

These groups are supervised in the same way as the other group activities, by a French psychologist.

Course of Treatment

The Armenian psychologist decides on the therapeutic strategy for each child received in consultation. He assures the follow-up treatment of the child and participates in weekly summary meetings that gather psychologists and educators, visitors and Armenians. They also decide when it is time for each child to leave the center, in collaboration with the teacher referring the child, if the child is participating in group activities. The treatments are brief; that is, a follow-up assessment consultation must take place at the latest after two months of treatment.

When a child is considered by everyone to be recovered and his or her departure from the center is decided, we routinely propose that the family come back one month later. This consultation enables us to evaluate the well-being of the child and of his or her family at a later time.

The entire course of the treatment is discussed in meetings and supervised by the French psychologist and educator.

Methodological Precautions

Besides anthropological library work, in Armenia we began to work with local anthropologists and anyone who could serve as a source of information (elementary-school teachers, nursery-school personnel, health-care professionals) in order to better adapt our work to their cultural universe. For example, we learned to identify, thanks to Armenian professionals, the cultural codes for the expression of suffering by children. Thus, children experience pseudo-hallucinations: they see souls, dead people. Many events are considered to be closely linked to Armenian traditions — most of the time these are cultural ways of expressing a difficult mourning process.

However, aware of the difficulty of transcultural work (Moro et al., 1989) and given the fact that this type of intervention was done for the first time within this framework, we wanted a modest project, first for a six-month period, with an evaluation of the results. Following this assessment, we decided to continue our work until July 1991. From that date the entire administrative, technical, and clinical responsibilities were assumed exclusively by the Armenian team we had trained. Following one year of autonomous operation, I returned there in July 1992 to make one final evaluation.

Operational Evaluation

Sources

I will present here only the main results concerning the evaluation of the operation of the center during the eighteen-month period we worked together. For this, I rely on three sources:

1. The analysis of all the monthly reports written by the team, reports that review the main indications for treatment (source: MSF).
2. The study of this mission made by A. Seiler (1992) for the Epicentre. This study was done with a sample of 329 charts drawn randomly from those that were available. A questionnaire was created in order to permit the study of the activities of the center. The analysis of this data was carried out with EPIINFO software (source: EPIINFO).

3. My own assessments made during my trips to Armenia (source: fieldwork).

Activities of the Center during the Eighteen-month Operating Period (December 1989 — June 1991)

Attendance at the Center   Figure 7-1 describes the number of monthly consultations carried out at the center (source: MSF). Consultations increased from April to July 1990 (with a maximum of 170 consultations during the month of June), and then decreased rapidly until October 1990 (a holiday period). They continued to decrease, albeit very slowly, in the following period.

Figure 7-2 plots the number of group sessions. There were two peaks during this period: 300 sessions during May 1990 and 400 in November 1991, following which the number of sessions slowly decreased.

Case Population (Seiler, 1992, provides further details)

The average age of the children is 8 years, 55.8 percent of the children are male, and 59 percent of the children go to school.

Figure 7.1 *Number of Monthly Consultations*

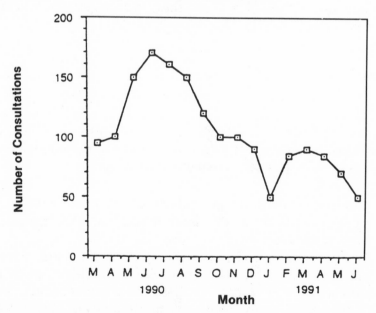

Note: In order to read this graph in detail, it is necessary to analyze the number of consultations in relation to vacations, to the number of psychologists present, to the difference between the children registered and present, and so on. Source: Seiler (1992). Reprinted by permission.

Figure 7.2 *Number of Group Activities Sessions*

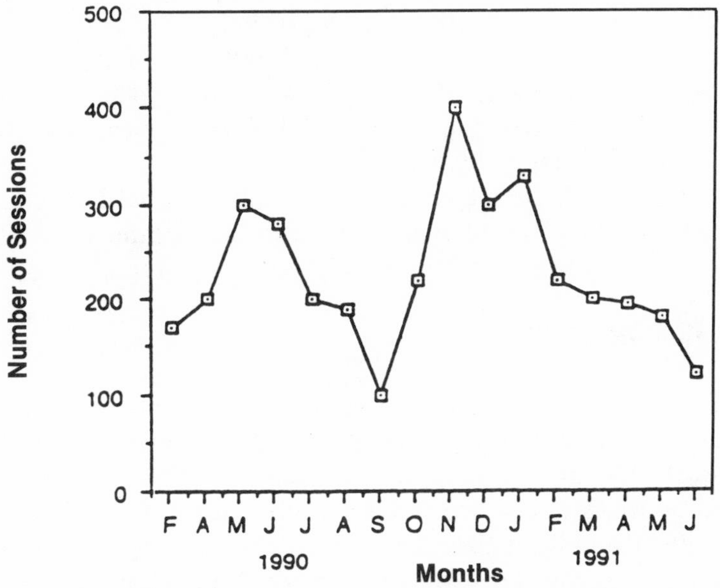

For methodological precautions, cf. Figure 7.1. Source: Seiler (1992). Reprinted by permission.

Forty-four percent saw their home destroyed, 31.2 percent live in a *doumik*, and 5.5 percent live with a relative; 10.7 percent have lost one or both parents.

Past medical and psychological histories reveal that 6 percent had previous psychological or psychiatric consultation during childhood, and 9 percent had neurological problems (basically epilepsy). Finally, 27.9 percent had difficulty becoming toilet trained during their childhood.

Children present with an average of three symptoms (see table 7-1) at the time of the first consultation. Five percent do not show any—the parents come for consultation to be reassured. Ten percent present with only one, 28 percent two, 31 percent three, 15 percent four, and 11 percent five or more.

Training

Training is provided in four ways: (1) training "while doing" consultations and group sessions (before and after each group session); (2) in the course of the weekly theoretical and clinical training session (theoretical discussion and analysis of situations); (3) during summary meetings that gather all the professionals together; (4) in the course of the weeks of active training — three weeks were set aside exclusively for training: one at the first consultation, another at the stressful situation and at the initiation of psychodrama, and the last one finally when discussing the stages of development of the child according to psychoanalytic theory. All of the training included a theoretical part, case studies, and supervised clinical work.

Among the different training methods proposed, evaluations have shown the efficacy of training at the same time as the clinical activity (following a consultation or after a group session).

Evaluation of Efficacy

After six months of operation, a first assessment showed the following: (1) good attendance at the center, which increased (100 in April, 150 in May); (2) good results from treatment, which lasted approximately two months (between the first consultation and when the child is considered to be recovered by the family and the team); (3) the speed with which the Armenian team acquired the skills necessary for this type of work.

Throughout eighteen months of working together, we saw operational modifications (duration of group sessions, supervision procedures, etc.). At the end of six months, the strictly reactive pathology seemed to decrease somewhat. Slowly, the teams started to broaden admission criteria and began to admit children who presented with fewer reactive and more chronic symptoms (psychological disturbances associated with epilepsy, neurotic disturbances, etc.).

As soon as the Armenian psychologist is comfortable with the procedure, the French psychologist is present at the consultations only if needed. From a constant presence, we move to an episodic presence, but systematic supervision continues (daily individual supervision, group supervision during weekly meetings, etc.). When a new psychologist joins the team, however, the process of systematic training and supervision starts again. The same procedure is used for the teachers.

The last six months were devoted to passing management responsibilities from the MSF center to the trained Armenian team. The center was placed under the direction of the Armenian ministry of education.

Our team continued to oversee periodic training. At the time of my evaluation, following one year of autonomous operation, I reported the following:

1. The center has good attendance (an average of 80 consultations and 100 group meetings per month).

2. Admission criteria have considerably broadened and include all neurotic pathologies; for example, the subgroup of the reactive pathology decreased, but remains, even during this period, at 20 percent. Therefore, three and a half years after the earthquake, reactive pathology continues, some children consulting only at this moment for disturbances that appeared after the earthquake. This must be underlined.

3. Psychologists and educators are more and more refined in their performance. They equip themselves with self-sufficient and reliable supervision methods and external training.

4. Finally, their technique is enriched by their own ideas.

Finally, in order to make explicit the specific situation we encountered, let us take a look at some sequences from a family treated at the center.

A CLINIC FOR TRAUMA, FEAR, AND MOURNING

Hermine came for consultation for her two children: Martin, 16 months, and Garen, 13 years. She was seen three times. Martin had been covered with eczema since the day after the earthquake. His mother said that everyone was afraid to touch him. His skin looked like scales.

Garen was afraid, having terrible and repetitive nightmares in which he saw details of the day of the earthquake (the elementary-school teacher says the word *bird* and at that moment the floor opens and the teacher disappears). The entire family (father, maternal grandmother, a 6-year-old sibling, uncles, aunts) died during the earthquake, except Hermine, Garen, and Martin. That day, Garen was in school. One of his friends was dead. His father and mother were at work; his father died under the rubble.

Following the first tremor, the mother left the cafeteria, running toward the nursery where Martin was. When she arrived there, she saw many children in the courtyard. She looked for Martin and could not find him. She recounts, "I arrived at the courtyard. I was under the impression that everything was black; then, I approached my son Martin and I had the impression that his face became full of light, like a halo around him; I extended my arm, and I was under the impression that my arm was too short to reach him. It was as if I was stuck to the ground and my arm was not long enough, and then I fainted. When I woke up, Martin was looking at me; again, I tried to touch him, but I couldn't."

After the earthquake, their life followed a rhythm dictated by the rituals of mourning. Garen, the older brother, said that he saw "spirits": "The spirits were big before; now they have become small and bright." Garen had been seeing these "spirits" for a long time, but after the earthquake, they became much more disturbing. His mother said that she knew that these "spirits" assail people who are sad.

If we looked at Martin in his mother's arms, we could see that she still held him on her knees. She held him by the tips of his fingers and by his buttocks. She did not cuddle him. After she put him on the floor, she often extended her hand up to a few centimeters from the buttocks of the baby, and then she stopped. In contrast, she made contact with Martin with her eyes.

A psychologist took the baby in her arms. She tried to establish some links with what had happened in the courtyard of the nursery at the time of the earthquake. The mother answered, "In any case, Martin is not the same since that day. It is as if he died and was then resurrected. At the beginning I was afraid that he would die; every night was as if I was watching over him." He slept in a small bed next to her, and she would wake up very often during the night and extend her arm toward him, and touch him. "I have made a sacrifice [a traditional Armenian rite]; now I am less frightened. I sleep, but sometimes I wake up frightened and I reach toward him."

She put the child on the floor, and mimicked the scene many times. But this time she did not repeat herself identically. She looked around at all the people present at the consultation, and supported by us, she delicately put her hand on the leg of her baby.

At the beginning of the consultation, Martin was hypotonic and overly reserved. His mother said that she did not know how to protect him. At this point, she felt enormous guilt about all her relatives who died during the earthquake, whereas she had the luck to remain alive. We noticed a distinct change in the quality of interactions with her baby during the meeting. The change took place at the moment she had the fantasy concerning the possible death of her baby during the night.

The rest of the work will consist of eliciting his mother's fantasies and exploring Garen's sadness by means of the drawings he does in between sessions. The traumatic dreams (dreams are important elements in Armenian traditional health-care systems) of both Hermine and Garen will be discussed in the consultation group, which will attempt to establish links between the elements of the dream and their concerns.

Mourning and trauma in the mother; sadness, trauma, and deprivation in the children will be repeated in a common story. Very rapidly, the symptoms will subside.

CONCLUSIONS

A question I have thought about for a long time is, How do children survive in crisis situations? I have taken this question to Pakistan, to the Afghan refugee camps, to South America, and then to Armenia many times. I will need, without a doubt, a thousand and one more trips. The successful experience in Armenia taught me one essential thing: psychic trauma is, of course, unavoidable within such tragedies, but we have at our disposal truly effective means to reduce the pain as long as we build, together with local people, a plan of action that will be rigorous and collaborative and where there will be room both for our own way of doing things and for the specific ways of the population concerned.

REFERENCES

Arménie-Diaspora. (1989). "Mémoire et modernité." *Les Temps modernes*, nos. 504, 505, 506.
Chiland, C., ed. (1983). *L'entretien clinique*. Paris: PUF.
Kasbarian-Bricout, B. (1984). *Les Arméniens au XXe siècle*. Paris: L'Harmattan.
_____ (1990). *Coutumes et traditions arméniennes*. Paris: L'Harmattan.
Médecins du Monde. (1989). Unpublished report, April 15.
Moro, M. R. (1992). "Les méthodes cliniques." In *Cours de Psychologie*, vol. 2, ed. R. Ghiglione and J. F. Richard. Paris: Dunod.

_____ (1993). *Parents en exil. Psychopathologie des interactions précoces*. Paris: PUF.

Moro, M. R., et al. (1989). "Le bébé dans son univers culturel." In *Psychopathologie du bébé*, ed. S. Lebovici and F. Weil-Halpern. Paris: PUF, 683–750.

Nouvelle Revue d'Ethnopsychiatrie. (1989). Grenoble, La pensée Sauvage, no. 12, "L'enfant exposé."

Nouvelle Revue d'Ethnopsychiatrie. (1990). Grenoble, La pensée Sauvage, no. 15, "Frayeur."

Seiler, A. (1992). *Etude de la mission pédo-psychologique Médecins sans Frontières*. Paris: Epicentre (Groupe européen d'expertise en épidémiologie pratique).

Verluise, P. (1989). *Arménie. La fracture*. Paris: Stock.

Winnicott, D. W. (1971). *Playing and Reality*. London: Tavistock.

8

Refugee Children and Violence

MARGUERITE E. MALAKOFF

INTRODUCTION

At the end of 1992, there were an estimated 16.6 million refugees worldwide (USCR, 1993). Children represent approximately half the refugee population—there are some 8 million displaced children (Office of the United Nations High Commissioner for Refugees, 1988). The fact that the children are still physically, emotionally, and cognitively immature and that they are rapidly *developing* makes their situation very different than that of adult refugees. They are probably the most vulnerable group in any refugee crisis. Refugee children are not just refugees—they are children whose healthy development is in jeopardy. Many refugee children from war-torn areas experience more trauma in a few years than many adults experience in a lifetime.

After resettlement, much is expected of these children. Refugee children are expected to adapt and adjust. They must learn a new language; adjust to a new culture; and define an identity that satisfies both their family and their new community. They must master the delicate art of juggling two sets of values. They assume the role of culture and language guide for the family. Refugee children are often assumed to be resilient—to be able to leave behind the trauma and start anew. Yet very little is known about the adjustment and long-term development of refugee children following the trauma of their flight and resettlement.

By definition, refugees are a political creation: the legal definition is both narrow and specific. The international legal definition of refugee status is laid out in the United Nations Convention Relating to the Status of Refugees (1951). It states that a refugee is

> any person who . . . owing to a well-founded fear of being persecuted for reasons of race, religion, nationality, membership of a particular social group or political opinion, is outside the country of his nationality and is unable or, owing to such fear, is unwilling to avail himself of the protection of that country. [art. 1 (A) (2)]

The determination of refugee status is thus a political and foreign policy issue, not a humanitarian one. Few governments recognize nonpolitical refugees, even in the face of natural or man-made disaster.

Recognized Refugees and Undocumented Immigrants

Given the legal nature of the definition of refugees, it is important to distinguish between legal refugees (as determined by the re-settlement country) and "illegal" refugees, considered to be illegal immigrants by most governments. The largest illegal refugee populations in the United States are Central Americans (in particular, Salvadoran) and Haitians. Salvadoran children are probably the largest group of refugee children in the United States to have experienced and fled war-related trauma. Practitioners estimate that at least half of the Salvadoran children in the United States have directly experienced war-related trauma.

Refugees and Displaced Persons

A second legal distinction that is important to keep in mind is that between international refugees, who have crossed an international border, and "displaced persons" who have remained within their country and therefore do not fall within the legal definition of a "refugee" regardless of the circumstances that caused their flight. Displaced persons are "refugees" within their own country and thus typically do not fall within the mandate of international agencies; hence, it is difficult to report on their numbers. The U.S. Committee on Refugees (USCR) estimates that there are some twenty-three million persons displaced as a result of human conflict or forced relocations. These populations share many characteristics with refugees who cross international borders, including the fact that they tend to include large numbers of women and children.

REFUGEE CHILDREN: A HETEROGENEOUS POPULATION

All too often, refugee children are viewed as a single population—perhaps not a homogeneous one, but one that shares more commonalities than differences. However, the needs of refugee children are not all the same. They have different cultures, languages, migration, premigration, and postmigration experiences.

Refugee children differ both by culture and by *wave* within a culture. Clearly, children from the Soviet Union are very different from children from Cambodia. However, even within a region the successive refugee waves will differ. The adjustment problems in the early eighties of the more rural Boat People arriving in the United State were a surprise because of the successful integration of 300,000 urban Vietnamese refugees in the mid-seventies.

The first wave of refugees to arrive from a given conflict are frequently the well-educated elite, who are often familiar with Western culture. Subsequent waves generally reflect a broader range of socioeconomic backgrounds, with a gradual lowering of the mean socioeconomic status and familiarity with urban and Western life. Later waves also frequently arrive with greater exposure to war-related trauma and refugee-camp experiences. In short, they are often both less well prepared for resettlement and more traumatized.

In addition to sociocultural differences, refugees also differ in terms of premigration and migration experiences. The Khmer are holocaust survivors; the Lao have spent long years in refugee camps; the Vietnamese have experienced war and political turmoil; Afghan children have fled suddenly over mountains; Salvadoran children have witnessed persecutions; Mozambican children have been child soldiers. Children may have been prepared for the departure, or, as often in the case of illicit escape, be given no warning or explanation until the escape is underway or completed. Each refugee crisis is different, and the experiences of individual children within the crises differ dramatically.

Some refugee families arrive in the United States or other Western countries equipped to deal with Western society; others arrive with little knowledge of what to expect. Some children arrive with Western-like educational experience; others have never been in a classroom. Children from war-torn countries do not have the same experience as children from countries where persecution is more subtle. Children who have spent long years in closed camps have very different preparation than children who have been part of a normal community while awaiting their final relocation.

REFUGEE CHILDREN AND VIOLENCE

Refugee crises are most frequently caused by situations of armed conflict that force large populations to flee. These are the situations in which children are especially vulnerable. In armed conflicts, children are likely to be exposed to the trauma of military conflict and political persecution prior to the flight. During large population movement, children are at high risk of being separated from their families, either through injury or death to a parent or through accidental separation. Large refugee crises frequently result in the establishment of first-asylum refugee camps, which are rarely able to meet the special needs of children. In the case of long-term refugee populations, it may be years before the mental health and educational needs of children are even partially addressed. In many cases, even the nutritional needs of children are never adequately met (Benjamin and Morgan, 1989; Garbarino et al., 1991; Mollica and Jalbert, 1989).

Political and armed conflicts also make refugee children vulnerable to political and military exploitation. Guns are being delivered to refugees in many parts of the world, and underage children are being trained to use them. In Peshawar, Pakistan, children were restricted to the camp and trained as resistance fighters until they were old enough to fight—usually their midteens (Boothby and Humphrey, 1987; Helsinki Watch, 1986); in Burma, children as young as 10 fight with the resistance (Stanley, 1990); and the

Khmer Rouge abduct children as young as 12 to serve as porters and soldiers (Reynell, 1988). Boothby and Humphrey (1987) suggest that parents' inability to protect their children from violence, illegal recruitment, and abduction has become a principal reason for refugee flight. They further note that nearly 90 percent of the casualties in the then current political conflicts were women and children.

Unaccompanied Minors

In emergencies, adults are the most important source of physical protection and emotional security. Younger children, especially, are dependent on older family members to provide a "safety zone" from the outside world. During war and refugee movements, unaccompanied children are especially at physical and psychological risk. They are the most vulnerable to malnutrition and preventable disease, which have killed millions of children in past refugee movements. They are vulnerable to abduction and forced participation in military actions, to rape, to exploitation (Kinzie et al., 1986; Ressler et al., 1988). And their vulnerability does not end when they reach a country of asylum: without the protection of adults, they are also at increased risk in refugee and displaced persons' camps (Comerford et al., 1991).

In their volume on unaccompanied children, Ressler, Boothby, and Steinbock (1988) note that it is important to distinguish between two broad types of separations: voluntary and involuntary. These types, defined from the perspective of the parents, in part define the situation of the child at separation and reunion. They suggest nine categories of separation within these two types. Involuntary separations may involve children who are abducted, lost, orphaned, runaway, or removed. Voluntary separations may involve children who are abandoned, entrusted to other adults, surrendered to authorities, or who are living independently. Situations of war are likely to produce unaccompanied children who fall into all nine categories, underscoring the fact that the situation of each unaccompanied minor is different.

Many children separated from their families during war and refugee movements are subjected to multiple levels of trauma and instability. Ressler, Boothby, and Steinbock (1988) summarize the sparse literature on the effects of separation compounded by war and refugee adversities. Children separated from their families tend to exhibit distress reactions that are related to age and developmental level. Distress reactions for children school-age and younger include withdrawal, depression, bed-wetting, sleep disturbances, restlessness, and behavioral problems (see also Hunt, 1988; Kinzie et al., 1986). Age at separation or loss appears to be an important factor in children's outcomes. Younger children seem to be more vulnerable to short- and long-term emotional distress than older children, presumably because older children possess more internal resources to cope with the separation (see Ressler et al., 1988, for review).

Several factors appear to mediate the intensity and duration of the emotional distress. One, already mentioned, is the nature of the separation. A second factor is the availability of alternative care following separation: when care that includes the opportunity both to form emotional bonds with other adults and to participate in developmentally appropriate social and educational activities is available immediately following separation, distress reactions are less likely to develop into long-term psychological disorders (see also Kinzie et al., 1986). A third factor is the nature of premigration and migration trauma. When separation is accompanied by exposure to violence, death, abuse, and hunger, the likelihood of adjustment problems and serious psychological disorders increases dramatically (see also Felsman et al., 1990; Kinzie et al., 1986).

Children in Refugee Camps: Humane Deterrence

Increasingly, refugee populations are being held in refugee camps in countries of first asylum—or even in their own countries, as is currently the case in Bosnia and Croatia. And yet, twenty years after the beginning of the Southeast Asian refugee crisis and when there are now children and teenagers who have known nothing or almost nothing but life in refugee camps, we still know little about the effects of such experiences on development. Refugee camps may be *open* or *closed*. Open camps allow refugees free access to the surrounding communities, and sometimes permit children to attend surrounding schools. In some cases, refugees are permitted to work in the nearby communities. Closed camps, which are far more common, restrict refugees to the camp compound, permitting only very limited access to the surrounding communities.

Many Southeast Asian refugees have spent months, usually

years, in camps of first asylum. With rare exception, these are closed camps designed to provide difficult living conditions, minimal nutrition and health services, and limited education. This policy, ironically termed *humane deterrence*, has much to do with deterrence and little to do with humane care.

With rare exception, the few Cambodian and Laotian children currently being resettled have spent close to ten years in closed camps — some their whole lives. Those resettled in the late eighties had generally spent at least four years in first-asylum refugee camps. These camps frequently add to the premigration trauma through overcrowded conditions, a culture of dependency, and lack of adequate educational and mental health services. There is a lack of adequate security, and children live in a climate of pervasive fear, stress, and depression (Benjamin and Morgan, 1989).

Children in Detention Centers: Hong Kong

An extreme case of closed camps are the detention centers in Hong Kong. In an attempt to deter the arrival of further refugees, Hong Kong set up "detention centers" in the late eighties. These are jail-like centers, some surrounded by barbed wire and metal sheeting, in which conditions are worse than in closed camps. They were designed to serve as processing centers and to hold those not admitted as refugees. However, given the processing time required for screening and the lack of a viable solution for those not accepted as refugees, they have become long-term detention centers for thousands of Vietnamese refugees. In 1991, there were some 16,000 children in detention, of whom 7,000 were under the age of 5. Close to 40 percent of the detainees are under the age of 17. Many of the children had spent more than three years in the detention centers. This population also included a sizable number of unaccompanied minors, many of whom left or were sent by their families to Hong Kong (Comerford et al., 1991).

The centers are overcrowded, and families are housed in bunk-like conditions. Families live side by side, separated only by planks and a thin curtain. There is no space and no privacy; children are exposed to everything that occurs within the hut or surrounding section. The majority of the detainees are Vietnamese Boat People who arrived in the late eighties. The prevalence of multiple piracy attacks during this period was such that most survivors of the trip will have witnessed the rape of women and young girls on board; and some will have survived the murder of their fellow passengers. All will have experienced extreme hunger and thirst (UNHCR, 1988; USCR, 1989).

In 1991, Refugee Concern Hong Kong, a group of refugee advocates and social workers, published a report on conditions inside the detention centers (Comerford et al., 1991). Their report focused on the condition of children in detention, which they described as a "developmental catastrophe." The report lists five areas of loss these children experience: physical and mental deprivation; loss of a safe environment and a sense of security; deterioration of family structure; malnutrition; and inadequate health care. They note that violence is pervasive within the centers, and many children will have witnessed their parents as well as strangers involved in acts of violence. The unaccompanied minors unanimously stated that their main concern in detention was violence and their safety. Many unaccompanied minors were recruited into gangs, which offer both protection and a sense of power.

The detention center conditions disrupt all aspects of the traditional family, culture, and religion. Restricted by the environment, parents are powerless to meet the needs of their children. Children's lives are governed by rules and regulations, which are arbitrarily enforced. They have virtually no space for recreation, and the educational program is limited. There are no mental health services, and only limited physical health services. Not surprisingly, social workers found high levels of emotional distress among the children. Both parents and service providers reported high levels of depression, aggressiveness, fear, anxiety, and nightmares among children of all ages.

Illegal Refugees: Central Americans in the United States

Political conflict in Central America produced a large population of traumatized children. Practitioners estimate that at least 50 percent of the Salvadoran children in the United States have experienced war-related trauma. The experiences of these children and adolescents prior to leaving Central America, the nature of the clandestine trip to the United States, and their undocumented status after arrival put them at special risk for emotional distress.

Children often arrive shell-shocked and fearful of authority.

According to a social worker at one impacted school system (personal communication, 1989), the children have been so warned against speaking during the trip that they will not talk during their first days or weeks at school. In some cases they have suffered physically and emotionally from neglect or intentional abuse at the hands of the smuggler. They may have been picked up and detained by border guards. In most cases they have walked long distances and have crossed the border under dangerous conditions. In some cases, children have been separated from their parents during the trip; in the worst cases, children have seen members of their family injured or killed during the voyage.

Because of their illegal status, undocumented children do not have access to most social services, although they are perhaps the children most in need of educational and psychosocial support. Practitioners familiar with Salvadoran children agree that the majority have witnessed violence and war trauma prior to leaving El Salvador. A survey of Salvadoran adolescents in the District of Columbia found that 81 percent of the adolescents interviewed had been exposed to at least one of six traumatic events: violent death, violent attack, rape, interrogation, imprisonment, torture. The survey further found that 65 percent of the youths reported being exposed to the violent death of at least one family member or friend, and 47 percent had been exposed to a violent attack on a family member or friend (Ito et al., 1987). Surveys of other Central American refugees have reported similar high levels of exposure to violence (Melville and Lykes, 1992; Rousseau et al., 1989).

A number of studies have reported high levels of emotional distress, and in particular, symptoms of post-traumatic stress disorder, among Central American populations. Ito et al. (1987) estimated that 30 to 50 percent of the adolescents surveyed might suffer from post-traumatic stress disorder (PTSD). A study of 8- to 12-year-olds with similar high levels of exposure found high levels of clinical symptoms that clustered around anxiety-depressive disorders (Rousseau et al., 1989). Arroyo and Eth (1985) found that 30 percent of the Central American youngsters they saw met PTSD diagnoses.

Displaced Persons: Thai-Cambodia Border Camps

By the late 1980s there were an estimated 300,000 displaced civilians housed in camps along the Thai-Cambodian border

(USCR, 1993). Defined, for political purposes, as displaced persons rather than refugees, they had lived in border camps since the early 1980s. By 1989, it was estimated that half of the camp population was under 15 and a third under the age of 5 (USCR, 1988). The majority of the children under the age of 10 knew nothing but the camps, and many young teenagers could remember little else.

Limited studies of camp conditions raise concerns about the developmental outcome of children brought up in such an environment. A 1989 study of mental health at the camps reported that there was a "widespread and deep-rooted mental health crisis" among camp residents (Mollica and Jalbert, 1989). The number of suicides had more than doubled in the two previous years, and 90 percent of the attempts were made by women between the ages of 15 and 30. A second survey found that the rates of induced abortions were increasing, child abuse was on the rise, and that domestic violence and rape were common (USCR, 1988). Violence was pervasive and an absence of security inside the camp led to a marked increase in levels of anxiety and depression. In addition to widespread physical violence within the camp, there were periodic shelling and attacks on the camp from the outside (Mollica and Jalbert, 1989; Reynell, 1988; USCR, 1988).

It is almost impossible to predict what the long-term effects of this situation will be on the children and adolescents who are now resettling Cambodia. For those who have known nothing but camp life, their available role models are adults who are demoralized, dependent on others to meet their needs, emotionally and physically traumatized, and use violence or are subjected to violence. Authority is based on power, and power on violence. Garbarino et al. (1991) reported that young mothers lacked role models and had to be taught mothering skills. Reynell (1988) found that children were being taught to lie and cheat to better their chances of survival in the face of limited resources.

RESEARCH ON REFUGEE CHILDREN: THE LONG-TERM EFFECTS

There is still little known about either the adjustment of refugee children or the effects of war-related trauma on children, and hence about the effects of war-related trauma on refugee children. Until recently, many of the larger studies looking at the adjustment of refugee youth focused on academic achievement, as this was of primary concern to the federal government (see for example, Caplan et al., 1989; Rumbaut and Ima, 1988). There have been few large-scale studies of the socioemotional adjustment of refugee children, either subsequent to resettlement or while in camps of first asylum.

There is much evidence suggesting that refugee children exposed to war-related trauma show symptoms of PTSD, depression, and other emotional disorders. Exposure to war leads to a heightened awareness of death, psychic numbing, and distrustfulness (Comerford et al., 1991; Garbarino et al., 1991; Garbarino et al., 1992; Melville and Lykes, 1992; Picado, 1988).

Studies of resettled Cambodian refugee youth have found long-term effects of exposure to extreme violence. Kinzie et al. (1986) interviewed forty adolescents who had lived through four years of the Pol Pot regime as children; the youth were interviewed four years after resettlement. They reported high levels of exposure to trauma: 83 percent had been separated from their families; 63 percent had seen persons killed; 18 percent saw family members killed; 68 percent had survived extreme starvation. Kinzie and colleagues (1986) report that 50 percent of the adolescents met *DSM-III* criteria for PTSD. Other diagnoses included major depressive order, intermittent depressive disorder, and anxiety disorder. Cambodian adolescents interviewed ten years after exposure to the Pol Pot regime as children also showed high levels of PTSD: 37 percent met the stricter *DSM-III-R* criteria and 83 percent met *DSM-III* criteria for PTSD (Realmuto et al., 1992). The main reason for not meeting the stricter *DSM-III-R* criteria was the absence of hyperarousal. Ninety percent of the youth reported both experiencing starvation and seeing dead bodies.

Children of victims of political persecution, in the absence of military conflict, also show high levels of emotional distress. Hjern et al. (1991) interviewed fifty-five Chilean children recently settled in Sweden, and compared children who had witnessed a "persecution event" with those who had not. The study found strong associations between experiences of persecution and introverted behaviors. Dependency was most common among preschool children, while concentration disorders were more common among school-age children. Hyperalertness and fears were frequently described by all children. A study of Chilean refugee children in Finland reported similar findings (Cohn et al., 1980).

Given the experiences of refugee children in war, it is remarkable that many children do recover emotionally and, in time, demonstrate normal and healthy development. The family appears to play an important role in providing an emotional buffer, both during migration and in the postmigration period. Refugee children who remain with or are rapidly reunited with their families or other emotionally available caretakers show less emotional distress and better adjustment than children who survive the refugee process alone (Garbarino et al., 1992; Masser, 1992; Melville and Lykes, 1992; Tsoi et al., 1986).

On the other hand, research on the adjustment of unaccompanied minors suggests that this population, once resettled, is still at heightened risk for adjustment problems. Rumbaut and Ima (1988) found that Vietnamese youth involved in gangs and other delinquent behavior were more likely to be living without one or both natural parents. Kinzie and colleagues (1986) found that of the fourteen unaccompanied minors they interviewed, thirteen met criteria for a psychiatric diagnosis. Hunt (1988) also found high levels of depression among resettled Vietnamese youth in foster homes.

CONCLUSIONS

Much more research is needed to examine both the short- and long-term effects of war and refugee-related trauma on children. Few studies have examined the effects of war-related trauma among refugee children, and those that do exist often have methodological problems (Athey and Ahearn, 1991). Many children who escape war-torn regions, and especially those who spend subsequent years in camps of first asylum, know little but varieties of violence and trauma. Loss is a defining characteristic of refugee status. For refugee children, it may mean the loss of their siblings and parents, in addition to that of their homes, their possessions, and their friends.

There is much to suggest that refugee children are a group that is, in developmental standards, multiply at risk. Minimally, they encounter a lengthy or permanent separation from their previous environment, are exposed to high levels of stress before and after resettlement, experience culture shock and isolation while they learn a new language, must learn to juggle two conflicting cultures, and experience a cultural separation between school and home. In addition, many live in low-income neighborhoods, have had to travel clandestinely, have experienced lengthy or permanent separation from one or both parents and/or siblings, have witnessed or experienced personal violence against someone they know, have suffered food deprivation, or have uneducated or poorly educated parents. In the mainstream population, any one of these factors is considered to put the child at risk for academic underachievement and mental health problems.

Most of the federal money allocated for educational services for refugee children is directed toward bilingual education programs and research on academic achievement. However, as Huyck and Fields (1981) noted over a decade ago, research focusing on language and academic progress "might well be the priority for immigrant children, but there is every reason to distinguish refugee children from other immigrants and to recognize that their generally unmet needs are health care (medical and psychological) and that the unit of service to children should be predominantly the family" (p. 254). Research since has only served to confirm this proposition.

Although photographs of refugee children are on the front pages of newspapers and on the covers of publications, the children's situation gets little attention. In the text, they are mentioned but in passing. Yet it is the children who are the most likely to see the end of long armed conflicts; it is the children who must build the future. In a special issue devoted to refugee children, UNHCR noted that although, numerically, half of the world's refugees are children, they are, being children, far more than half the world's responsibility (UNHCR, 1988).

REFERENCES

Arroyo, W., and Eth, S. (1985). "Children Traumatized by Central American Warfare." In *Posttraumatic Stress Disorder in Children*, ed. S. Eth and R. S. Pynoos. Washington, D.C.: American Psychiatric Press.

Athey, J. L., and Ahearn., F. L. (1991). "The Mental Health of Refugee

Children: An Overview." In *Refugee Children: Theory, Research, and Services*, ed. F. L. Ahearn and J. L. Athey. Baltimore: Johns Hopkins University Press.

Benjamin, M. P., and Morgan, P. C. (1989). "Refugee Children Traumatized by War and Violence: The Challenge Offered to the Service Delivery System." In *Conference on Refugee Children Traumatized by War and Violence*. Washington, D.C.: CASSP Technical Assistance Center; Georgetown University Child Development Center.

Boothby, N., and Humphrey, J. (1987). "Under the Gun—Children in Exile." In *World Refugee Survey, 1987*, ed. USCR. Washington, DC: American Council for Nationalities Service.

Caplan, N., Whitmore, J. K., and Choy, M. H. (1989). *The Boat People and Achievement in America: A Study of Family Life, Hard Work, and Cultural Values*. Ann Arbor, Mich.: University of Michigan Press.

Cohn, J., Holzer, K. I., Koch, L., and Severin, B. (1980). "Children and Torture." *Danish Medical Bulletin* 27(5): 238–239.

Comerford, S. A., Armour-Hileman, V. L., and Waller, S. R. (1991). *Defenseless in Detention*. Hong Kong: Refugee Concern Hong Kong.

Felsman, J. K., Leong, F. T., Johnson, M. C., and Felsman, I. C. (1990). "Estimates of Psychological Distress among Vietnamese Refugees: Adolescents, Unaccompanied Minors, and Young Adults." *Social Science & Medicine* 31(11):1251–1256.

Garbarino, J., Dubrow, N., Kostelny, K., and Pardo, C. (1992). *Children in Danger: Coping with the Consequences of Community Violence*. San Francisco: Jossey-Bass.

Garbarino, J., Kostelny, K., and Dubrow, N. (1991). *No Place to Be a Child*. Lexington, MA: Lexington Books.

Hjern, A., Angel, B., and Hojer, B. (1991). "Persecution and Behavior: A Report of Refugee Children from Chile." *Child Abuse & Neglect* 15(3):239–248.

Hunt, D. J. (1988). "The Adaptation of Southeast Asian Refugee Children after Resettlement in the United States." Paper presented at Conference on Refugee Children Traumatized by War and Violence, Bethesda, MD, 28–30 September.

Huyck, E. E., and Fields, R. (1981). "Impact of Resettlement on Refugee Children." *International Migration Review* 53/54:246–354.

Ito, T. K., Campos, R., and Harrington, D. (1987). *Summary and Preliminary Results of the Adolescent Salvadoran Health and Psychosocial Survey*. Washington, D. C.: Mayor's Office on Latino Affairs.

Kinzie, J. D., Sack, W. H., Angell, R. H., et al. (1986). "The Psychiatric Effects of Massive Trauma on Cambodian Children: I. The Children." *Journal of the American Academy of Child and Adolescent Psychiatry* 25(3):370–376.

Laber, J. (1986). *To Win the Children: Afghanistan's Other War.* Helanki Watch/Asia Watch.

Masser, D. S. (1992). "Psychosocial Functioning of Central American Refugee Children." *Child Welfare* 71(5):439–456.

Melville, M. B., and Lykes, M. B. (1992). "Guatemalan Indian Children and the Sociocultural Effects of Government Sponsored Terrorism." *Social Science & Medicine* 34(5):533–548.

Mollica, R. F., and Jalbert, R. R. (1989). *Community of Confinement: The Mental Health Crisis in Site Two.* Alexandria, VA: Committee on Refugees and Migrants, World Federation for Mental Health.

Picado, J. M. (1988). *The War in El Salvador.* Ph.D. Diss. University of Southern California.

Realmuto, G. M., Masten, A., Carole, L. F., et al. (1992). "Adolescent Survivors of Massive Childhood Trauma in Cambodia: Life Events and Current Symptoms." *Journal of Traumatic Stress* 5(4):589–599.

Ressler, E., Boothby, N., and Steinbock, D. (1988). *Unaccompanied Children: Care and Protection in Wars, Natural Disasters, and Refugee Movements.* New York: Oxford University Press.

Reynell, J. (1988). *Political Pawns; Political Pawns: Refugees on the Thai-Kampuchean Border.* Oxford: Refugee Studies Program.

Rousseau, C., Corin, E., and Renaud, C. (1989). "Conflit armé et trauma: une étude clinique chez des enfants refugiés latino-américains." *Canadian Journal of Psychiatry* 34(5):376–385.

Rumbaut, R., and Ima, K. (1988). *The Adaptation of Southeast Asian Refugee Youth: A Comparative Study.* Final report to the Office of Refugee Resettlement. Washington, DC: U.S. Department of Health and Human Services.

Stanley, A. (1990). "Child Warriors." *Time,* 18 June, 30–52.

Tsoi, M. M., Yu, G. K., and Lieh-Mak, F. (1986). "Vietnamese Refugee Children in Camps in Hong Kong." *Social Science & Medicine* 23(11):1147–1150.

United Nations. (1951). *Convention Relating to the Status of Refugees.* Geneva, Switzerland: United Nations.

United Nations High Commissioner for Refugees (UNHCR). (1988). "Guidelines on refugee children." Interoffice memorandum no. 91/88, field memorandum no. 85–88. Geneva, Switzerland: Office of the High Commissioner for Refugees.

_____ (1988). Refugee Children. *Refugees:* No. 54, June.

U.S. Committee for Refugees. (1988). *Refugee Reports* 9(7).

_____ (1989). *Refugee Reports* 10(5), May.

_____ (1993). "1992 World Refugee Statistics." In *World Refugee Survey 1993.* Washington, D.C.: American Nationalities Council.

IV

Violence in the Child's Culture

How do we conceptualize the violence in the child's world that will lead to his or her becoming a violent adult — do the major factors lie in the family and local community, unaffected by larger cultural features, or does the nature of the child's culture affect the likelihood that he or she will become a violent adult? Is it possible to identify widespread cultural influences that are so pervasive and severe that their effects on a child's later aggressive behavior can be predicted? For example, can broad political, economic, and social systems influence the lives of children in a manner that leads to identifiable effects on the development of aggression in children?

Our attitudes toward aggressive violence can be complex, even contradictory, which might serve as another cultural source of violent behaviors in children. Are these contradictions codified in the laws of a nation, or do they appear only in the implementation of the laws? At what point do the contradictions become permissive in their message, facilitating violent attitudes in children? Can an understanding of the history of specific laws help us understand how a people's attitude toward aggression determines how individuals subsequently behave? Do laws truly embody attitudes toward violence that differ across cultures? Do they influence child-rearing practices and affect the individual's behavior as an adult?

Some cultures control the expression of aggression among youth, while others are more permissive. The latter are skeptical about possible cultural stimulation of violent attitudes in children and leave responsibility to families. Is there any method by which we can learn how cultural attitudes toward aggression, the written or unwritten rules about aggressive behavior, are transmitted to our children? Do we know how they learn about aggression and its uses, and how early in childhood? Are there harmful cultural influences transmitted to children that encourage their later violent aggression that could be relatively easily changed? Can they be convincingly demonstrated? Do we permit cultural influences that interfere with the right of children to develop self-control?

Finally, can the disparate and incomplete information available now help us to minimize the development of aggressive, violent behaviors in children? Have we clear ideas about what causes aggressive behavior and how to prevent it?

9

Sociocultural Roots of Violence: Street Children in Brazil

SALVADOR CELIA

I stopped stealing and using drugs because I began to go to a Community Center. At first I went there to eat, then I began to participate in activities and meetings.

> *M.A.S., a street child*
> *(Folha de São Paulo, a newspaper,*
> *22 November 1992)*

Yo soy yo y mis circunstancias
(I am myself and my circumstances)

> *Ortega y Gasset*

This old phrase by Ortega y Gasset is still up to date, especially when we look at the situation of the so-called *meninos de rua* (street children) or *meninos na rua* (children in the street), who roam the cities of Brazil in large numbers. Brazil, however, is not the only country in this sorry condition, and the increased violence today in several countries of the world, especially in large cities, alarms society as a whole. Yet, unfortunately, society does not change its attitude and find effective solutions to this sad problem. Inadequate government policies — for instance, massive public investment in favored economic sectors to the detriment of social programs — have caused some countries enjoying high gross national products to suffer a simultaneous sharp drop in indices of the quality of life. Thus, in several countries, the rich become richer and the poor poorer.

SOCIAL NEGLECT AND SOCIAL VIOLENCE

Recently, John Kenneth Galbraith, in his excellent book, *The Culture of Contentment* (1992), made a prediction of what might happen in the large cities of the United States, including an escalation of violence, which did in fact occur and will certainly occur again.

According to Galbraith, the present model of American society, with little investment in basic human values (such as general welfare, homes, leisure and community centers, education, and health care), brings society to a state of internal explosion. The situation is so serious that unless a severe crisis takes place, such as that of the thirties, the United States will be unable to find a way out. Such is his despair regarding the present political system that the last chapter of his book is entitled "Requiem."

When these phenomena occur in Third-World countries the results are more immediate and dramatic. This is the case in Brazil today. Known for its natural beauty and high cultural and economic potential, Brazil has gained a reputation for violence (especially in some cities). Former centers of tourist attraction and sources of foreign currency are now considered hostile, to be avoided by the international community. In some places, group violence and ganglike actions no longer spare even the wonderful beaches. Some of these aggressive actions are delinquent, others anarchical, an expression of revolt intended to frighten and deprive other people of their leisure.

Social violence does not appear overnight. It is a worry to everyone because of the frightening forms it takes; among the worst are the genesis of a legion of children who do not receive even basic necessities, including food. Pathetically, 31 percent of children below the age of 6 in Brazil are undernourished. Millions of these children do not stand a chance, do not have a "voice" to express themselves, because their apathetic, passive behavior is invisible when compared with the restless, dramatic street children, who at least manage to resist ill-organized policies that prevent appropriate social welfare.

In 1985, according to official statistics, the status of the Brazilian population between zero and 19 years of age was as follows: they constituted 63 million people (47 percent of the total population), 36 million of whom (57 percent of the youth) were underprivileged; 7 million (20 percent of the underprivileged youth) had been abandoned; and 427,000 were inmates of institutions, of whom 6,000 were delinquents.

Therefore, over half the Brazilian children may be considered underprivileged, which stimulates an essential question: How can 57 percent of the children in a country be relegated to living untouched by circulating comfort and wealth, and excluded from life and official history? These figures, quoted by Ligia Costa Leite (1991), give rise to a second observation, that they are mainly black, with habits and customs different from those considered conventional for society by the dominant culture.

In Brazil 140 million of the almost 150 million inhabitants live in poverty or complete misery. Recent figures from the Brazilian Institute for Geography and Statistics show that 1 percent of the population receives 14.6 percent of the income; 75 percent of workers earn less than U.S. $150 a month. It is surprising to recall that this occurs in the country with the eighth largest gross national product in the world. However, income concentration alone cannot explain the problems of the country.

In 1940 Brazil had a population of 41 million. Today it is close to 150 million. The last decades have been a social tragedy. Agricultural modernization caused the migration of 30 million people between 1960 and 1980; consequently, 42 percent of the population was absorbed by ten large urban centers. Feudal structures persisted in the hinterland, with large, unproductive properties. If we compare the capitalist vision of countries such as the United States, Japan, France, and England with the "false capitalism" of Brazil, we see that the latter gave priority to export policies and underwent the paradoxical situation of going hungry while exporting food to other countries. These economic problems generated the *favelas* (slums) and their sad psychological consequences. Finally, since 1980 the country's economy has been in severe recession. The sum of all these factors led to an explosion of violence. It is estimated that in 1989, fifty thousand murders occurred in Brazil, the same number as the total of all American soldiers killed in Vietnam.

STREET CHILDREN IN BRAZIL

As a consequence of these factors, there was a brutal drop in the quality of life of Brazilians, markedly influencing the growth and development of their children. One of the problems resulting from this social tragedy is the street children. There are two subgroups. The first is characterized by antisocial behavior, no home, no shelter, and no family; they make the street their home. The second group consists of boys and girls for whom the street is a workplace for their families and themselves; they return home at night.

A so-called empty house syndrome has been described. It refers to a place where no relatives or adult figures exist, and the house is simply a place to sleep. But the people are not solitary. They form a grouping (cluster), rather than a social group, in which forces may interact to provide greater security and confidence for the individual. In most of them a father figure is missing, and the mothers have already had three or four male partners. Obviously, there is a loss of roots and bonds in these families, leading to very poor interaction, with consequent problems in personality development. Children who survive such an unfavorable social environment are denied values, feelings, and potential by the elite, and their behavior arises in response to what has been given or denied them. Survivors of this deteriorating "quality of life" are considered "invincible" by Leite (1991). She sees their form of survival as a type of magic.

For these boys and girls the streets retain the aura of happiness, pleasure, and freedom instead of the unhappiness attributed to them. That is why, at the first chance, they run away from shelters, homes, reform schools, and so forth, as a way of calling attention to the segregation that is imposed on them. In Brazil they are the heirs of the black culture, of Zumbi (the king) and his followers in the Quilombo dos Palmares. Quilombos were settlements of escaped black slaves. The blacks fought the battles of their communities, using the *capoeira* (a dance and fighting sport) to face slavery and obtain the human rights that had been withheld from them. The behavior of these street children began in the slave quarters and quilombos that so tormented, and still torment, the authorities, frightening society. It was formerly seen as a national security problem; today it tends to be considered a pathology associated with criminal activity. Actually, it appears to demonstrate the healthy aspect of the "invincibles," when, as a form of resistance to imposed rules and domination, the children use creativity to survive in a world hostile to their culture, values, and color. The lack of a core family is compensated for by the vitality of the group, which does not segregate the child among children, but includes him or her in the battle for survival.

PREVENTION AND INTERVENTION IN THE COMMUNITY: STRATEGIES IN PORTO ALEGRE

A society that lives with few protective or mediating supports, and many risk factors, exposes these children to significant psychosocial trauma, which generates profound problems in personality development. The results of this trauma depend on the intensity, duration, and time at which it affects the child.

Protective factors play an essential role in prevention. The typical profile of these children and adolescents indicates that it is very difficult for them to establish attachments, due to their poverty and lack of attention from their families, beginning during fetal life. A woman, especially when pregnant, does not receive any attention from the health-care system, although she should have at least four checkups during pregnancy; only exceptionally will ultrasonography be performed. Furthermore, few women receive psychological support, either individually or as a group, in this difficult phase of life with deep physical and social changes.

In a successful experiment with community participation, we established groups for low-income pregnant women, creating conditions that focused them on their pregnancies and facilitated attachment with the children when they were born. These women were seen after delivery and during the infant's first year of life to assess the development of sociability in these babies, as compared with the control group, which consisted of babies whose mothers had not received this support. Encouraging breast-feeding in health campaigns, taking care not to hurt and cause guilt feelings in women who do not breast-feed, has also helped to improve infant development.

It is useful to mention our work in Porto Alegre at Vida Centro Humanistico, providing care to a 300-family *favela,* where the percentage of undernourished children, between the ages of zero and 3 years, was 21 percent. Malnourishment, a national tragedy, was assessed to find the true profile of these families and mothers, and to improve our understanding of the phenomenon and establish action strategies. It was found that the mothers of undernourished children, as compared with the control group, were people who had lost their roots, migrated from the hinterland. did not have the support of their husband or partner, and usually did not desire the pregnancy. Some had wanted and even attempted abortion, and most had suffered experiences of abandonment, neglect, or abuse. They had intense depressive feelings (100 percent were depressed according to the Beck Scale), and the mean time of breast-feeding was 51 days, as compared with 250 days in the control group. This study supports the concept that while undernourishment is a nutritional disease, it contains many elements of affective and bonding disorders.

The strategy employed in our work was to provide integrated, multidisciplinary care within the home, or in a small house called the Nutrition Center, built by the community. Generally, preventive care comes from recovering substitute figures such as grandparents, uncles, aunts, or even neighbors who empathize with the children. By accepting care in neighbors' houses, they receive the attention of a good caregiver; whenever possible, they are placed in community nurseries, but there are unfortunately far too few of these. The follow-up of infant growth and development in community or health centers, as individual or parent–infant group care, may provide a motivating element for the conservation or reinforcement of attachment, besides the importance of observing development and parent–infant interactions.

Another crucial factor for social bonding is school. School is considered the great route to social ascension in many countries, especially in highly competitive societies. But, in other countries, school no longer is a happy place where one learns to become someone important tomorrow: it is often filled with frustration and rejection. In Brazil, as reported in *Why Children Reject School* (Celia, 1990), it has become a source of rejection and avoidance, and no longer protects development. The country fails to give a real priority to education, a low professional value is ascribed to teachers, and there are inadequate curricula; the result is that 50 percent of children and adolescents now remain away from school. Rethinking education and school is an essential requirement for democratic societies that believe in the importance of education in building citizenship and self-esteem.

Setting up humanistic centers, places dedicated to life projects, antidotes to a society full of death projects, is another possibility for caring for human beings and improving the quality of life. In our experience in Porto Alegre, an old ceramics factory located in a poor neighborhood, which was to have become a model prison, was instead transformed into a real "factory" of life projects. The center is managed by the government and by community organizations constituting a community council. For the last two years it has worked through projects and social policies to build up citizenship and reinforce self-esteem. There are now sixty-eight projects to prevent illness and promote health, and to provide cultural and professional training, sports and leisure, and an introduction to science and technology. Priority is given to citizens' rights, in general, and to women who are victims of violence, in particular. Based on three generations of the community, the center makes an effort to integrate different fields, providing special care to high-risk babies, the handicapped, street children, women who have been raped, and the aged. At the same time, it supplies a supportive atmosphere for all those in the community who come there, without distinction. It may be seen, symbolically, as a spider web, resistant and flexible, holding and giving creative motivation to generate more autonomous, independent, creative individuals.

MASSIVE CHALLENGES AND HOPEFUL FUTURES FOR CHILDREN

By reinforcing protective factors and reducing the risk factors of misery and poverty, rethinking the political aspects of society, reviewing the economy, improving income distribution, satisfying basic human needs regarding individual citizenship, favoring bonding, and reducing frustrations while offering better conditions, we may arrive at a state of hope. Thus, knowing that we will have a better life, we may build a country, a more humane world, in which children will no longer be on the streets and will enjoy their rights to citizenship and self-esteem.

REFERENCES

Celia, S. (1990). "School Refusal and School Problems in Brazil." In *Why Children Reject School: Views from Seven Countries,* ed. C. Chiland and J. G. Young. New Haven: Yale University Press.

Celia, S., Alves, M., Behs, B., et al. (1992). *Malnutrition and Infant Development*. Presented at the Fifth International Congress of the World Association for Infant Psychiatry and Development, Chicago, U.S.A.

Celia, S., Santos, A. M., Krowczuk, E., et al. (1983). "Assistência materno-infantil. Análises de uma experiência. Perspectivas." In *A criança e o adolescente brasileiro da década de 80*. Porto Alegre, Brazil: Editora Artes Médicas, 13–28.

Chicago Sun-Times. (1992). "As killings near record, city looks for reasons." 13 September.

Folha de São Paulo. (1992). 22 November.

Dimenstein, G. (1992). "Os nossos meninos que Deus os tenha." *Revista Imprensa*, no. 6:14–21.

Galbraith, J. K. (1992). *La cultura de la satisfacción*. Buenos Aires: Emecê.

Green, M., and Haggerty, J. R. (1992). "Pediatria e adaptação." In *Pediatria Ambulatorial*, Porto Alegre, Brazil: Editora Artes Médicas.

Leite, L. C. (1991). *A magia dos invencíveis*. Rio de Janeiro: Editora Vozes, Petrópolis.

Moura, W. (1992). "A familia contra a rua." In *O trabalho e a rua*, chap. 7, São Paulo, Brazil: Cortez Editora.

10

American Violence, American Values, and Childhood Games

R I C H A R D   M A X W E L L   B R O W N

The family of Dwight D. (Ike) Eisenhower moved to Abilene, Kansas, from Texas when he was one year old. Far in the future of this lad who grew up in Abilene, Kansas, was his command of the armies of America and its allies in Western Europe during World War II and, later, his presidency of the United States. Abilene was a remarkable town for an impressionable youngster like Ike. The Abilene of Ike's childhood years of 8 to 13 was only thirty years from the frontier era of glory when the town was the renowned destination of longhorn cattle driven up the Chisholm Trail from Texas. From the stockyards of Abilene the ill-fated longhorns were shipped by rail to the packing plants of the Midwest. The wild years of Abilene from the late 1860s to the early 1870s were years when rambunctious cowboys up from Texas were on the shoot and avid for pleasure after months of dusty service herding cattle north. In Abilene and other famous Kansas "cattle towns" of the time such as Dodge City, Caldwell, and Wichita, the Texas cowboys were an unruly element whose trade was welcomed by the local merchants but whose violence was not. The solution to the problem of preserving order in Abilene and similar boomtowns of the Great Plains was the two-fisted, fast-firing marshal who could outshoot and overawe the tough Texas cowboys. The prototypical frontier marshal of the era was James Butler (Wild Bill) Hickok, who served as marshal of Abilene in 1871. One of Hickok's most famous kills came in Abilene—an episode in which in a point-blank gun duel he downed a Texas troublemaker, gambler, saloon keeper, and famed gunfighter, Phil Coe. As an 8-year old being reared in Abilene with its heritage of notable frontier violence, Ike Eisenhower knew all about the gunfighting exploits of the town's greatest hero, Wild Bill Hickok, who had been hired by the town fathers to preserve order and decorum at the point of a revolver.

Indeed, Wild Bill Hickok was a particular idol of Ike in the years from 1898 to 1903 when Ike was 8 to 13 years old. Ike knew about Wild Bill not just from dime novels but from the tales of Abilene old-timers from the Hickok era of only three decades before—old-timers who knew Wild Bill, remembered his Abilene moment of gunfighting glory, and were articulate about it all to wide-eyed boys like Ike and his brother, Edgar Eisenhower. As boys in their preteen years, Ike and Edgar were fascinated by the famous gunfighters who roamed about Kansas and the West, and they whiled away their after-school hours by playing "Wild West" games. In their childhood play Ike and Edgar favored quick-draw gunfighter games in which they impersonated their heroes, Bat Masterson, Billy the Kid, Jesse James, and—greatest of all to them—their hometown idol, Wild Bill Hickok.

Dwight D. Eisenhower's hero worship of Wild Bill Hickok and the legendary gunfighters of the West was no passing childhood fancy but a lifelong fascination. By the time Eisenhower died he had long since himself become one of America's greatest heroes of the twentieth century for his military leadership against the armies of Hitler and his presidency of the United States during the 1950s at the peak of the nation's worldwide power. Aside from history and biography, President Eisenhower's favorite reading was about the Old West in the form of Westerns—novels about the frontier and its mythic gunfighters that he read for entertainment and escape from his heavy duties as the prime American leader of the "Free World" in its Cold-War vendetta against worldwide Communism headed by Soviet Russia. At Ike's bedside in his Gettysburg, Pennsylvania, home where he died were six Zane Grey novels. Another author of Westerns favored by Ike was Max Brand (the pseudonym of Frederick Faust), and Eisenhower's favorite product of Hollywood was the classic Western film *High Noon* (1952), starring Gary Cooper as the triumphant gunfighter.

By the time Dwight D. Eisenhower became president of the United States, his boyhood admiration for Wild Bill Hickok was undiminished and not hidden from the nation. In a nationally televised speech of 1953 President Eisenhower specifically cited

Hickok as a role model whose quality of forthright courage as a gunfighter was to be emulated by Americans. As the president spoke into the television camera, he told his nationwide audience that as a boy in Abilene he had been reared to "prize" the ethical code of frontier Abilene and "our marshal," the eminent gunfighter, Wild Bill Hickok. The president still believed in the code of Abilene and of Hickok, which, he proudly declared, was to "meet anyone face to face with whom you disagree" and "if you met him face to face and took the same risk he did, you could get away with almost anything as long as the bullet was in front." By "almost anything" Ike meant killing in an honorable cause.

Who was Wild Bill Hickok—this figure in the American past so admired by the nation's midcentury leader of the Free World—and for what values did Wild Bill stand? Hickok was certainly no myth. His life as a gunfighter and plainsman had a hard reality that was tested time and again by the defining moment of gunfire with, as Eisenhower said, the bullet always in front. More than any other single person, Wild Bill Hickok established the social institution of the "walkdown"—beloved of the writers and filmers of Westerns but something that was a frequent reality in frontier Western life—in which two armed men with itching trigger finger and hostile intent stride down a dusty Western street ready to draw, fire, and settle their differences in an archetypal showdown. Wild Bill Hickok was the real-life star in a walkdown that— although probably not the first such episode was one of the earliest and the one that gained national publicity and immeasurably helped create a Western tradition—occurred in Springfield, Missouri, in 1865 not long after the end of the Civil War. By serving as a scout, spy, and detective on the side of the Union armies in the bloody Civil War fighting of Missouri and Arkansas, James Butler Hickok had gained his enduring nickname of Wild Bill. By July 1865, when the walkdown in Springfield occurred, Hickok had four years before established his broader reputation as a champion of gunplay. In Springfield his rivalry with one Dave Tutt was both political and military. Hickok had grown up in northern Illinois in a strong abolitionist family, and his father operated a secret stop on the Underground Railroad—a route along which slaves could travel from bondage in the South to freedom in Canada. Ideologically, the mature gunfighting Hickok was an ardent member of the Republican Party and a fighter for the Union cause in the Civil War. Dave Tutt, on the other hand, had fought for the Confederacy in the Missouri-Arkansas region and hated his acquaintance Hickok's politics. Thus, politics and ideology heightened by a personal dispute brought the well-armed Hickok and Tutt face to face across the courthouse square of Springfield on 21 July, 1865.

In the late afternoon of 21 July shadows from the massive courthouse and the surrounding elms lengthened over the huge three-acre public square of Springfield. Hogs seeking relief from the summer heat wallowed in mud holes. Loungers about the hitching racks and stores around the square were alert — they had heard tales of threats exchanged by Tutt and Hickok. What these witnesses to the West's precedent-setting walkdown saw was the following: Having left the Lyon House, a hotel a block away, Wild Bill entered the square and paced from its southeast corner toward Dave Tutt, who came out of a livery stable and headed straight for his opponent Hickok. "Don't come any closer, Dave!" was Wild Bill's warning and challenge. Heedless and unafraid, Tutt drew his gun. At about 50 to 75 yards, both men fired almost at the same time, although the deadly Hickok may have gotten off his shot an instant sooner. As Tutt's bullet whistled overhead, Hickok's typically sure aim pierced his opponent's heart. Two years later this locally famous but otherwise obscure episode of violence gained national prominence as America's and the West's prototypical walkdown in a lavish story that appeared in the nation's favorite monthly magazine, *Harper's*. This article by reporter Henry M. Stanley (later to earn global notoriety for his successful search in Africa for the missing explorer, Dr. David Livingstone) made Wild Bill Hickok an instant American celebrity. Stanley extolled Hickok's gunfighting triumph over Tutt and became the first of what would be a growing list of leading figures — including General Custer, for whom Hickok served as a scout in his warfare with Great Plains Indians in the late 1860s — to voice their admiration of Hickok. On the basis of his gunfighting skill demonstrated against Dave Tutt, Hickok went on a few years later to become the model, as noted above, of the quick-draw, fast-firing town marshal and preserver of the peace in the boomtowns of Kansas and the West — until the end of Wild Bill came in 1876 when, without warning, he was shot in the back by a Deadwood, Dakota Territory, culprit.

In the realm of American values, Wild Bill Hickok stood for the concept of no-duty-to-retreat violence: a mode of aggressive self-defense that during the nineteenth century was enshrined in

American law and society and that today is still a widely held American social value—one that suffuses the national history, myth, and psyche. Hickok's face-to-face no-duty-to-retreat style of killing Dave Tutt in 1865 and Phil Coe (in Abilene in 1871) was confronted by a courtroom trial and vindicated by a jury of his peers in the aftermath of his fatal shooting of Tutt.

A few weeks after killing Tutt, Wild Bill was arrested and charged with murder. Being tried on the reduced charge of manslaughter, Hickok's plea of self-defense was resisted by the trial judge, who invoked the legal obligation of the "duty to retreat" (Hickok certainly had neither attempted to escape from Tutt nor retreat from him). The judge, reported a Springfield newspaper, "instructed the jury to the . . . effect" that Hickok "was not entitled to an acquital [*sic*] on the ground of self-defense unless he was anxious to *avoid the fight*, and used all reasonable means to do so" [emphasis added][1]—one of which would have been to flee from the scene, for Hickok, should he have chosen it, had a wide-open route of escape from the killing site. The jury, however, saw Hickok as a "true man" who rightfully stood his ground, for, continued the newspaper report, "the jury seems to have thought differently" than the judge and in rejecting the judge's doctrine of the duty to retreat found Wild Bill not guilty.

In focusing on the issue of retreating or standing one's ground in a situation of violent individual combat, the judge in the trial of Wild Bill Hickok touched directly on a key trend in American society and American values. During the late 1960s a wave of riots, assassinations, and turmoil led President Lyndon B. Johnson to appoint a National Commission on the Causes and Prevention of Violence. Since then, assassinations (at this writing) have waned, but the American homicide rate has climbed steadily to reach the all-time high level of the 1980s and 1990s. The national nemesis of homicide is, however, nothing new but is deeply embedded in the American tradition. Largely overlooked has been a vital legal transformation that played a significant role in our role as a homicide-prone country and that has gained us the unenviable status as the nation with by far the highest homicide rate among our peer group of the modern, industrialized democracies of the world: that is, the replacement of the ancient English common-law requirement of the duty to retreat in a potentially

---

[1]Springfield *Missouri Weekly Patriot*, August 10, 1865.

homicidal situation with the American common-law doctrine of standing one's ground against a hostile opponent. The most vigorous growth of the new nineteenth-century American right of no duty to retreat was in the frontier states west of the Appalachian Mountains.

As far back as the thirteenth century, English common law dealt harshly with the act of homicide. "The right to kill in self-defense was slowly established, and is a doctrine of modern rather than medieval law," wrote Joseph H. Beale in the *Harvard Law Review* in 1903. In his eighteenth-century *Commentaries* on English common law, Blackstone favored the centuries-long bias of common law against killing in self-defense out of his concern that the right to defend might be mistaken for the right to kill. Crucial to English common law regarding homicide was the notion of escape: in a personal dispute that threatened to become violent, one must flee from the scene. Should it be impossible to get away, however, common law required that one retreat as far as possible—"to the wall" at one's back was the legal phrase—before violently resisting an antagonist in an act of lawful self-defense.

Thus, in English society of the medieval and early-modern periods, the Crown through its courts attempted to reduce the incidence of homicide by shifting personal disputes from field and street to the judicial chamber. At its nub, the duty to retreat was a command to individuals to forsake physical conflict. There were, of course, many fewer situations in which flight from the scene was entirely blocked, and even in such cases individuals had to retreat until they could retreat no further (to the wall at one's back) before standing their ground and, if necessary, killing in self-defense. Compared with the United States, England has long had a much lower homicide rate, and surely one reason has been England's still deeply rooted doctrine of the duty to retreat.

Two of the most influential state supreme court decisions in the legal process of establishing the American doctrine of no duty to retreat in our law and society came in 1876–1877 in the "true man" and "American mind" decisions from Ohio and Indiana. In the Ohio case, *Erwin v. State* (1876), James W. Erwin had been convicted of second-degree murder because, according to the trial judge's instruction, he had not obeyed the duty to retreat before killing in self-defense when he had stood his ground and shot to death an ax-wielding opponent. Contrary to the lower court, the Ohio Supreme Court held that a "true man" (the assumption was that there was—or should be—no other kind of man) was "not obliged to fly" from an assailant and that, therefore, there was no duty to retreat from a menacing assailant in Ohio. In neighboring Indiana one year later a similar case came before the state supreme court. In *Runyan v. State* (1877) the Indiana Supreme Court roundly repudiated the traditional English duty to retreat, and in a key passage that was to be widely quoted in other state supreme court decisions reversing the duty to retreat, stated that "*the tendency of the American mind* seems to be very strongly against the enforcement of any rule which requires a person to flee [or retreat] when assailed" [emphasis added]. In effect, the Indiana Supreme Court held that the duty to retreat was a legal rationale for cowardice and that cowardice was simply un-American. With a majority of American state supreme courts (especially those west of the Appalachians) having endorsed the new American common law doctrine of no duty to retreat, the United States Supreme Court waffled until it definitively ruled on the issue of retreat or no retreat in the 1921 case of *Brown v. United States*. The noted civil libertarian, Justice Oliver Wendell Holmes, wrote the Supreme Court's 7–2 opinion in favor of no duty to retreat declaring in measured tones on this case of homicide that came out of the state of Texas, "that if a man reasonably believes that he is in immediate danger of death or grievous bodily harm from his assailant he may *stand his ground* and that if he kills him he has not exceeded the bounds of lawful self-defense" [emphasis added]. So Holmes spoke in public in the chambers of the Supreme Court, but in private he spoke much more emotionally of his dislike of the notion of the duty to retreat (or flee) when he wrote, approvingly, that "it is well settled" in Texas that "a man is not born to run away."[2] Both publicly and privately Justice Holmes spoke for widely held public opinon in America. The attitude of no duty to retreat has deeply permeated our foreign relations, military habits, civilian pursuits, and childhood games such as those once played by the brothers Dwight D. and Edgar Eisenhower.

[2]See *Holmes-Laski Letters: The Correspondence of Mr. Justice Holmes and Harold J. Laski, 1916–1935* (2 vols. Cambridge, MA: Harvard University Press, 1953), ed. M. D. Howe, vol. 1, pp. 335–336.

11

Television and the Development of the Superego: Pathways to Violence

BRANDON S. CENTERWALL

In *Civilization and Its Discontents* (1930), Freud identified inhibition of violent impulses as one of the primary functions of the superego: "Civilization therefore obtains mastery over the individual's dangerous desire for aggression by weakening it and disarming it and by setting up an agency within him to watch over it like a garrison in a conquered city" (pp. 123–124). With a few exceptions (e.g., Klein, 1933, 1934), it has been the consensus that Freud was right and that, allowing for individual exceptions, persons committing acts of major violence suffer from superegos that are defective, deficient, or even completely absent.

In the classic psychoanalytic paradigm, the superego derives from the child's introjection of the parent through the process of identification. This was always a simplified picture of reality, since the child is busy introjecting all other significant personae as well. Nevertheless, it was understood that under the normal conditions of a nuclear family—one or two parents, one or more children—the parental introjects are by far the most important and therefore the classic model of superego formation a reasonable approximation of reality.

We no longer live under normal conditions. For the last forty years, the nuclear family has not been what it was. It has been expanded, and now consists of one or two parents, one or more children—and a television set. The dimensions of this change can be sketched out: American preschool children, ages 2 to 5 years old, watch an average of over twenty-seven hours of television per week (A.C. Nielsen Company, 1990); approximately half of American parents have given up setting limits on what their children watch on television or how much (Gallup and Newport, 1990); 24 percent of American households keep a television set in the child's bedroom (Peter D. Hart Research Associates, 1992); 13 percent of adult Americans describe themselves as addicted to television (Gallup and Newport, 1990); 25 percent of adult Americans cannot conceive of a sum of money large enough to persuade them to stop watching television (Peter D. Hart Research Associates, 1992).

Given its massive, daily presence, it might be suspected that chronic exposure of children to television could have some effect on superego formation. Curiously, however, the issue has not been addressed in the psychoanalytic, psychiatric, or psychological literature. Within the present chapter, I discuss television's effects within the context of normal child development; give an overview of natural exposure to television as a cause of aggression and violence; summarize my own research findings on television as a cause of violence; and then return to the theoretics of television and the development of the superego. The chapter ends with suggestions for action.

TELEVISION IN THE CONTEXT OF NORMAL CHILD DEVELOPMENT

The impact of television on children is best understood within the context of normal child development. Neonates are born with an instinctive capacity and desire to imitate adult human behavior. That infants can, and do, imitate an array of adult facial expressions has been demonstrated in neonates as young as a few hours old, that is, before they are even old enough to know cognitively that they themselves have facial features that correspond with those they are observing (Meltzoff and Moore, 1983, 1989). It is a most useful instinct, for the developing child must learn and master a vast repertoire of behavior in short order.

Whereas infants have an instinctive desire to imitate observed behavior, they do not possess an instinct for gauging a priori whether a behavior ought to be imitated. They will imitate anything (Meltzoff, 1988a), including behaviors that most adults would regard as destructive and antisocial. It may give pause for thought, then, to learn that infants as young as 14 months of age demonstrably observe and incorporate behaviors seen on television (figure 11–1; Meltzoff, 1988b, 1992). Writers and producers

Figure 11.1 *This series of photographs shows a 14-month-old boy learning from a television set. In photograph A the adult pulls apart a novel toy. The infant leans forward and carefully studies the adult's actions. In photograph B the infant is given the toy. In photograph C the infant pulls the toy apart, imitating what he saw the adult do. Sixty-five percent of infants exposed to the instructional video could later work the toy, compared with 20 percent of infants who were not exposed. Photo by A. N. Meltzoff (1992); reprinted by permission.*

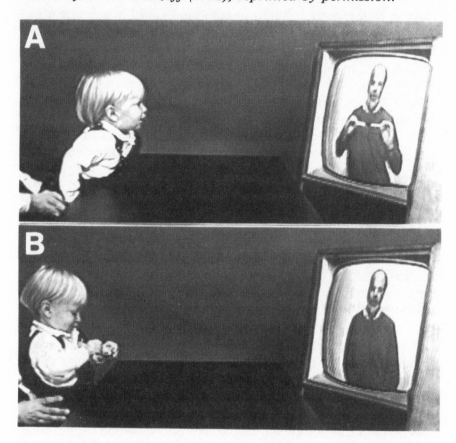

are well aware of this: a glance at television industry trade journals reveals sellers hawking their ability to attract and hold viewers as young as 2 years old. (Looking ahead, in two surveys of young male felons imprisoned for committing violent crimes, for example, homicide, rape, and assault, 22 to 34 percent reported having

Figure 11.1 *(continued)*

consciously imitated crime techniques learned from television programs, usually successfully [Heller and Polsky, 1976].)

Up through ages 3 and 4 years, many children have not yet operationalized the difference between fact and fantasy in television programs and remain unable to do so despite adult coaching (Flavell 1986). In the minds of such young children, television is a source of entirely factual information regarding how the world works. Naturally, as they get older, they come to know better, but the earliest and deepest impressions are laid down at an age when children see television as a factual source of information about a world outside their homes where violence is a daily commonplace and the commission of violence is generally powerful, exciting, charismatic, and efficacious. In later life, serious violence is most likely to erupt at moments of severe stress—and it is precisely at such moments that adolescents and adults are most likely to revert to their earliest, most visceral sense of what violence is and what its role is in society. Much of this sense will have come from television.

Not all laboratory experiments and short-term field studies (three months or less) demonstrate an effect of media violence on children's behavior, but most do (Andison, 1977; Hearold, 1986). In a recent meta-analysis of randomized, case-control, short-term studies, exposure to media violence caused, on the average, a significant increase in children's aggressiveness as measured by observation of their spontaneous, natural behavior following exposure (p < 0.05; Wood et al., 1991).

NATURAL EXPOSURE TO TELEVISION AS A CAUSE OF AGGRESSION AND VIOLENCE

In 1973, a small Canadian town (called Notel by the investigators) acquired television for the first time. The acquisition of television at such a late date was due to problems with signal reception rather than any hostility toward television. Joy and colleagues (1986) investigated the impact of television on this virgin community, using as control groups two similar communities that already had television. In a double-blind research design, a cohort of forty-five first- and second-grade students were observed prospectively over a period of two years for rates of objectively measured noxious physical aggression (e.g., hitting, shoving, and biting). Rates of physical aggression did not change significantly among children in the two control communities. Two years after the introduction of television, rates of physical aggression among children in Notel had increased by 160 percent (p < 0.001).

In a prospective study conducted from 1960 to 1981, Eron and Huesmann (1984) followed a complete age cohort of 875 children living in a semirural U.S. county. It was found that the frequency of television viewing at age 8 years predicted the seriousness of criminal acts committed by age 30. Children who were watching television frequently at age 8 on the average were convicted by age 30 of criminal acts several times more serious than the criminal acts of adults who had been infrequent viewers of television at age 8 (figure 11-2). This held true for both men (p < 0.001) and women (p < 0.05). The "seriousness" of a criminal act was weighted to reflect the severity of violence involved, using a standardized scale (Rossi et al., 1974). After controlling for the boys' baseline aggressiveness, intelligence, and socioeconomic status at age 8, it was found that the boys' television violence viewing at age 8 significantly predicted the seriousness of the crimes for which they were convicted by age 30 (p < 0.05; Huesmann, 1986).

In a retrospective case-control study, Kruttschnitt and colleagues (1986) compared 100 male felons imprisoned for violent crimes (e.g., homicide, rape, and assault) with 65 men without a

Figure 11.2 *Relationship of television viewing frequency at age 8 to seriousness of crimes committed by age 30. Columbia County Cohort Study, 1960–1981.*
Reprinted by permission from Eron and Huesmann (1984).

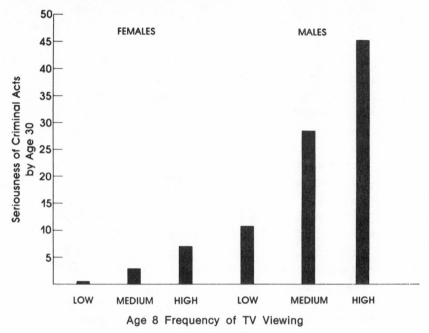

history of violent offenses, matching for age, race, and census tract of residence at age 10 to 14 years. After controlling for school performance, exposure to parental violence, and baseline level of criminality, it was found that the association between adult criminal violence and childhood exposure to television violence approached statistical significance ($p < 0.10$).

All Canadian and U.S. studies of the effect of prolonged childhood exposure to television (two years or more) demonstrate a positive relationship between earlier exposure to television and later physical aggressiveness, although not all studies reach statistical significance (Centerwall, 1989). The critical period of exposure to television is preadolescent childhood. Later variations in exposure, in adolescence and adulthood, do not exert any additional effect (Hennigan et al., 1982; Milavsky et al., 1982). However, the aggression-enhancing effect of childhood exposure to television is chronic, extending into later adolescence and adulthood (Centerwall, 1989). This implies that any interventions should be designed for children and their caregivers rather than for the general adult population.

These studies confirm what many Americans already believe on the basis of intuition. In a national opinion poll, 43 percent of adult Americans affirm that television violence "plays a part in making America a violent society," and an additional 37 percent find the thesis at least plausible (Harris, 1977). But how big a role does it play? What is the effect of exposure to television on entire populations? To address this issue, I took advantage of an historical experiment—the absence of television in South Africa prior to 1975 (Centerwall, 1989).

TELEVISION AND HOMICIDE IN SOUTH AFRICA, CANADA, AND THE UNITED STATES

The South African government did not permit television broadcasting prior to 1975, even though South African whites were a prosperous, industrialized Western society (Centerwall, 1989). Amid the hostile tensions between the Afrikaner and English white communities, it was generally conceded that any South African television broadcasting industry would have to rely on British and American imports to fill out its programming schedule. Afrikaner leaders felt that that would provide an unacceptable cultural advantage to the English-speaking white South Africans. Rather than negotiate a complicated compromise, the Afrikaner-controlled government chose to finesse the issue by forbidding television broadcasting entirely. Thus, an entire population of two million whites—rich and poor, urban and rural, educated and uneducated—was nonselectively and absolutely excluded from exposure to television for a quarter century after the medium was introduced into the United States. Since the ban on television was not based on any concerns regarding television and violence, there was no self-selection bias with respect to the hypothesis being tested.

To evaluate whether exposure to television is a cause of violence, I examined homicide rates in South Africa, Canada, and the United States. Given that blacks in South Africa live under quite different conditions than blacks in the United States, I limited the comparison to white homicide rates in South Africa and the United States and the total homicide rate in Canada (which was 97 percent white in 1951). Data analyzed were from the respective government vital statistics registries. The reliability of the homicide data is discussed elsewhere (Centerwall, 1989).

Following the introduction of television into the United States, the annual white homicide rate increased by 93 percent, from 3.0 homicides per 100,000 white population in 1945 to 5.8 homicides per 100,000 in 1974; in South Africa, where television was banned, the white homicide rate decreased by 7 percent, from 2.7 homicides per 100,000 white population in 1943 to 2.5 per 100,000 in 1974 (figure 11-3). As with U.S. whites, following the introduction of television into Canada, the Canadian homicide rate increased by 92 percent, from 1.3 homicides per 100,000 population in 1945 to 2.5 per 100,000 in 1974 (figure 11-4).

For both Canada and the United States, there was a lag of ten

Figure 11.3 *Television ownership and white homicide rates, United States and South Africa, 1945–1973. Asterisk denotes six-year average. Note that television broadcasting was not permitted in South Africa prior to 1975.*
Reprinted by permission from Centerwall (1989).

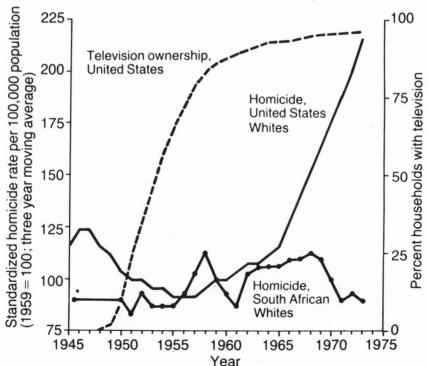

Figure 11.4 *Television ownership and homicide rates, Canadians and white South Africans, 1945–1973. Asterisk denotes six-year average. Note that television broadcasting was not permitted in South Africa prior to 1975.*
Reprinted by permission from Centerwall (1989).

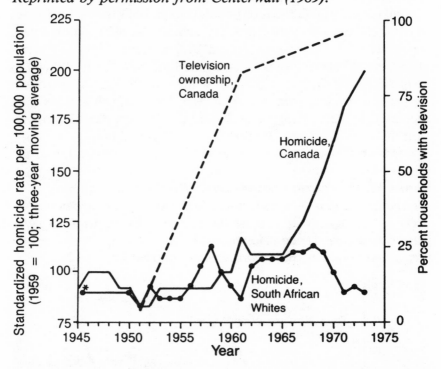

to fifteen years between the introduction of television and the subsequent doubling of the homicide rate (figures 11–3 and 11–4). Given that homicide is primarily an adult activity, if television exerts its behavior-modifying effects primarily on children, the initial "television generation" would have had to age 10 to 15 years before they would have been old enough to affect the homicide rate. If this were so, it would be expected that, as the initial television generation grew up, rates of serious violence would first begin to rise among children, then several years later it would begin to rise among adolescents, then still later among young adults, and so on. And that is what is observed (Centerwall, 1989).

In the period immediately preceding the introduction of television into Canada and the United States, all three countries were multiparty, representative, federal democracies with strong Christian religious influences, where people of nonwhite races were generally excluded from political power. Although television broadcasting was prohibited prior to 1975, white South Africa had well-developed book, newspaper, radio, and cinema industries. Therefore, the effect of television could be isolated from that of other media influences. In addition, I examined an array of other factors — changes in age distribution, urbanization, economic conditions, alcohol consumption, capital punishment, civil unrest, and the availability of firearms (Centerwall, 1989). None provided a viable alternative explanation for the observed homicide trends. For further details regarding the testing of the hypothesis, I refer the reader to the published monograph (Centerwall, 1989).

A comparison of South Africa with only the United States (figure 11-3) could easily lead to the hypothesis that U.S. involvement in the Vietnam War or the turbulence of the civil rights movement was responsible for the doubling of homicide rates in the United States. The inclusion of Canada as a control group precludes these hypotheses, since Canadians likewise experienced a doubling of homicide rates (figure 11-4) without involvement in the Vietnam War and without the turbulence of the U.S. civil rights movement.

There remains a residual concern that despite controlling for all of these factors there may exist yet another, unidentified factor that could account for the findings. It is not scientifically possible to prove a negative (i.e., I cannot prove that such a variable does not exist). Therefore, the theory that exposure to television causes violence must be subjected to further testing. Falsifiable hypotheses must be put to the test to determine whether the results substantiate or contradict the theory.

We begin with the observation that different populations within the United States acquired television at different times. Therefore, if the introduction of television in the 1950s indeed caused a subsequent doubling of the homicide rate, those populations that acquired television earlier should have had an earlier increase in their homicide rates, and those populations that acquired television later should have had a later increase in their homicide rates.

For example, as might be expected for what was then an expensive luxury commodity, minority households acquired their first television sets approximately five years later than white households (Centerwall, 1989). If the introduction of television did cause a doubling of the homicide rate, the white homicide rate should have begun to increase approximately five years before that of blacks and other minority groups. White homicide rates began to increase in 1958; as predicted by the hypothesis, the homicide rate of blacks and other minorities did not begin to increase until 1962, four years later (figure 11-5).

Similarly, the nine U.S. census regions did not acquire television at the same time. Neither did their homicide rates increase at the same time (Middle Atlantic, NY, PA, NJ, homicide rates began to increase in 1958, whereas West South Central, AR, LA, OK, TX, homicide rates did not begin to increase until 1964). The correlation between the timing of a region's acquisition of television and the timing of the region's subsequent increase in the homicide rate was 0.82 (p = 0.003; Centerwall, 1989).

As would be expected, major metropolitan centers acquired television first, followed by progressively smaller cities and towns. As predicted by the hypothesis, there was a parallel sequence in the increase in homicide rates, with the rates first increasing in the major metropolitan centers, then in progressively smaller cities and towns.

When I published my original paper in 1989, I predicted that white South African homicide rates would double within ten to fifteen years after the introduction of television in 1975, the rate having already increased 56 percent by 1983 (the most recent year then available). By 1987, the white South African homicide rate had reached 5.8 homicides per 100,000 white population, a 130 percent increase in the homicide rate from the rate of 2.5 per 100,000 in 1974, the last year before television was introduced (Central Statistical Service, 1989). (As of 1991, the South African vital statistics registry no longer distinguishes death certificates by race.)

In contrast, Canadian and white U.S. homicide rates have not increased since 1974. As of 1987, the Canadian homicide rate was 2.2 per 100,000, as compared with 2.5 per 100,000 in 1974 (World Health Organization, 1989). In 1987, the U.S. white homicide rate was 5.4 per 100,000, as compared with 5.8 per 100,000 in 1974 (National Center for Health Statistics, 1990). Since Canada and the United States became saturated with television by the early 1960s (figures 11-3 and 11-4), it was expected that the effect of television on rates of violence would likewise reach a saturation point ten to fifteen years later.

It is concluded that the introduction of television in the 1950s caused a subsequent doubling of the homicide rate, that is, long-term childhood exposure to television is a causal factor

Figure 11.5 *Change in homicide rate, by race of victim: United States, 1955–1981 (1955 = 100; three-year moving average). Source: National Center for Health Statistics. Reprinted by permission from Centerwall (1989).*

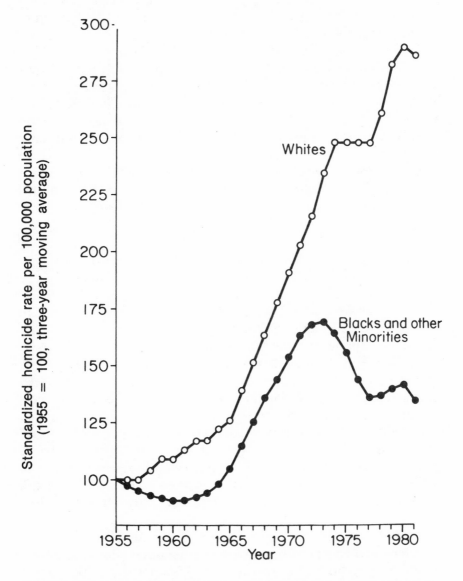

behind approximately one-half of the homicides committed in the United States, or approximately ten thousand homicides annually. Although the data are not as well developed for other forms of violence, they indicate that exposure to television is also a causal factor behind a major proportion — perhaps one-half — of rapes, assaults, and other forms of interpersonal violence in the United States (Centerwall, 1989). When the same analytic approach was taken to investigate the relationship between television and suicide, it was determined that the introduction of television in the 1950s exerted no significant effect on subsequent suicide rates (Centerwall, 1990).

To say that childhood exposure to television and television violence is a predisposing factor behind half of violent acts is not to discount the importance of other factors. Manifestly, every violent act is the result of an array of forces coming together — poverty, crime, intoxication, stress, conflict — of which childhood exposure to television is just one. Nevertheless, the evidence indicates that if, hypothetically, television technology had never been developed, there would today be 10,000 fewer homicides each year in the United States, 70,000 fewer rapes, and 700,000 fewer injurious assaults (Johnson and DeBerry, 1990).

TELEVISION AND THE DEVELOPMENT OF THE SUPEREGO

So how does exposure of children to television lead to acts of violence in later life? It has been amply demonstrated that children respond to the violent role models of television by becoming more aggressive themselves (Comstock and Paik, 1991; Wood et al., 1991). It has also been demonstrated that children exposed to television violence become desensitized to real violence, remaining passive in the presence of aggressive acting out and thereby permitting violent situations to escalate out of control (Drabman and Thomas, 1974). But these are the reactions of children. Why would an adult with a healthy superego revert to such behavior? To ask the question, however, is to assume that a child raised on television enters adulthood with a healthy superego.

As indicated by the opening quote, Freud (1932) saw the superego as an agent of tyranny. Although he certainly recognized that the superego is also the carrier of life's positive values, it was the sadistic, hypertrophied superego he wrote about: "The superego seems to have made a one-sided choice and to have picked out only the parents' strictness and severity, their prohibiting and punitive function, whereas their loving care seems not to have been taken over and maintained" (p. 62). This was probably because Freud had a vigorous superego of his own and his patient population was weighted with obsessives and melancholics. Then as now, antisocial persons with deficient superegos were unlikely to present for analysis. Be that as it may, later writers have generally followed Freud's lead and pondered the superego's unpleasant aspects far more than its positive functions (Post, 1972).

Consider persons without superegos: they have violent impulses like you and I, ego competence to carry out those impulses, and no reason they can see not to do so. Life is limited to the satisfaction of immediate appetite. Relationships serve only to meet the needs of libido and loneliness; as soon as those needs have been temporarily met, the relationship ceases to signify. Family and community exist only to be exploited; they neither comfort nor sustain. Work is only a means and provides no satisfaction. There is no creativity, no sense of individual identity, no sense of purpose or meaning. Since it is not possible to maintain for long a state of appetitive repletion, much of daily life is a vague emptiness and despair. There are no standards, no plans, no hopes, and therefore, of course, no future.

Under the normal conditions of a nuclear family, children avoid such a fate by means of the parental introject, provided the parent is a good source for the introjection of the ego ideal. Not surprisingly, the characteristics of a good source are the same characteristics we associate with a good parent:

1. A good parent manifests a coherent and consistent set of values. What that set of values is matters much less than that they be coherent and consistent.

2. A good parent protects the child, thereby validating to the child that the parent's values are worth something.

3. A good parent enforces standards, disciplining the child to the concept that there are standards.

4. A good parent is "there" for the child, providing an individualized, nurturing support attentive to the child's anxieties and needs. This support introjects into a nurturing and supporting superego structure.

As children individuate they may come to make their parents' values their own, or they may react against those values, but either way they will enter adulthood with a healthy, effective superego.

As noted, in the modern, extended nuclear family, the average American preschool child is watching a television set in excess of twenty-seven hours per week (A. C. Nielsen Company, 1990). If television, as a member of the family, is considered as a source for the introjection of the ego ideal, certain deficiencies become apparent:

1. The set of values presented to the child by television is not merely incoherent and inconsistent but is, in fact, completely chaotic. Flicking through the channels with the remote control exposes the child to as many different value systems as there are channels. A child cannot be expected to synthesize these contradictory presentations into an intelligible and stable value system of his or her own.

2. Television has not the slightest capacity to protect the child from anything. Values unaccompanied by protective force invite contempt.

3. Television is unable to enforce any value that it presents. In fact, it is the child—not television—who sets the terms of discourse. If the child does not care for the values being expressed, the child can change those values by flicking to another channel or end the values by blanking the set out. Even the most spineless parents are not *that* spineless.

4. Television is not only "not there" for the child, it is absolutely not there. Television does not care for the child, does not sense the child, does not respond to the child. The child knows this.

In sum, television is not merely a poor source for the child seeking to shape an ego ideal, it actively disrupts the process of superego formation, increasing the likelihood that the child will enter adulthood with a superego that is weak and poorly organized. Violence follows.

What draws the child to introject television in the first place? Spitz (1958) described three primordia of the later superego. First, from the first year of life the child is drawn to imitate behavior — not just the parents' behavior, but also that of siblings, strangers, animals, machinery, and, indeed, almost anything that can be described as having a behavior. Second, from the child's birth, the parents are, wittingly or not, shaping and conditioning the child's behavior, molding the child from an animal into a human being.

Imitation by the child and shaping by the parents form the seedbed of superego development.

The third primordium emerges during the second year of life, when the child comes to focus his or her identifications upon the parent through the process of identification with the aggressor. Parents may not wish to see themselves as "the aggressor," but under normal circumstances they are the young child's greatest source of anxiety, due to the parents' necessary role in frustrating the child's desires. The infant copes with this anxiety by identifying with the parents' ability to frustrate the infant. Children learn the magic of saying "No," and practice this new power on their parents, on everyone else, and most important, on themselves. This is not yet a superego, but it is the ontological precursor of the superego they will develop several years later.

Television fits into these primordia. First, it provides an endless stream of behavior for the child to imitate, and the child is imitating television at as young as 14 months old (figure 11–1). Second, television actively shapes and conditions the child's behavior by enticing the child to watch and then rewarding the child for continuing to watch. The child's imitation of television and the shaping of the child by television form the necessary base for the later introjection of television by the child.

Finally, television competes well with parents as a source of anxiety in the child, but through different means. Parent's provoke anxiety in children by frustrating their desires. Television provokes anxiety by exposing children to numerous scenes of physical and psychological violence, disconcerting juxtapositions and discontinuities, and simply much that is confusing, contradictory, and inappropriate to a child's level of psychological development. Every parent has had to deal with nightmares and fears generated by television, but that is only the tip of it, since most of the anxieties created by television are not articulated by the child to the parent. The child copes with this anxiety in the same manner as before, that is, by identification with the aggressor — in this case, television. Provoking anxiety in the child is not, of course, a primary intent of those who create television products, but the result is that the child introjects television as a means of coping with the anxiety. The child's identification will naturally be with those aspects of television that provoked anxiety.

Imitation of television; shaping by television; introjection of television. Children are finally launched into the inadequacies of superego development that flow from their use of television as an introject from which to develop an ego ideal. It has been demonstrated that long-term exposure of preadolescent children to television is a major cause of violence in later life. It could be concluded that television is not suitable for preadolescent children.

WHAT TO DO ABOUT IT

The American Academy of Pediatrics recommends that pediatricians advise parents to limit their children's television viewing to one to two hours per day, equivalent to a 50 percent reduction from current average viewing levels (American Academy of Pediatrics, 1990). This is an excellent point of departure and can be extended to anyone who works with parents and children. Children's exposure to television and television violence should be part of the agenda of child psychologists, child psychiatrists, and related mental health professionals.

Limiting children's exposure to television is one approach. A different tack can be taken as well by teaching children to master television. Mastery is control. When the child masters television, television no longer controls the child. In practice, this means teaching the child how television works, why it works, who is working it, and to what ends. A key element is giving children hands-on experience in using a television camera to create their own programs based upon their own creativity, their own needs, their own concerns. With the right equipment, this can be done in schools, in clinics, in community centers, and even in private homes. Media literacy education, as it is called, is a burgeoning field. Recent publications include *Visual Messages: Integrating Imagery into Instruction* (Considine and Haley, 1992) and *Parenting in a TV Age* (Davis et al., 1991). The latter has received the endorsement of the American Academy of Pediatrics.

Interestingly, it has been the experience of those teaching the hands-on use of television technology that it is those young people most alienated from the educational process who become most engaged in the mastery of television. It is as though *watching* television embodies their sense of passivity and pointlessness, whereas *making* television turns it all around. When a young person scanning the world with a television camera was asked how she felt, she said, "I feel in control." When a young man viewed the television program he had participated in as writer, actor, cameraman, and production editor, he said, "I see myself." These were things they had never experienced before with television.

REFERENCES

A. C. Nielsen Company. (1990). *Nielsen Report on Television 1990*. Northbrook, Ill.: Nielsen Media Research.

American Academy of Pediatrics, Committee on Communications. (1990). "Children, Adolescents, and Television." *Pediatrics* 85:1119–1120.

Andison, F. S. (1977). "TV Violence and Viewer Aggression: A Cumulation of Study Results, 1954–1976." *Public Opinion Quarterly* 41:314–331.

Centerwall, B. S. (1989). "Exposure to Television as a Cause of Violence." In *Public Communication and Behavior*, vol. 2, ed. G. Comstock. Orlando, Fla.: Academic Press, 1–58.

Central Statistical Service. (1989). *Deaths: Whites, Coloureds and Asians, 1987*. Pretoria, South Africa: Government Printer.

Comstock, G., and Paik, H. (1991). *Television and the American Child*. San Diego, Calif.: Academic Press.

Considine, D. M., and Haley, G. E. (1992). *Visual Messages: Integrating Imagery into Instruction*. Englewood, Colo.: Teacher Ideas Press.

Davis, J. F., Osborn, B., and Thoman, E. (1991). *Parenting in a TV Age*. Los Angeles, Calif.: Center for Media and Values.

Drabman, R. S., and Thomas, M. H. (1974). "Does Media Violence Increase Children's Toleration of Real-Life Aggression?" *Developmental Psychology* 10:418–421.

Eron, L. D., and Huesmann, L. R. (1984). "The Control of Aggressive Behavior by Changes in Attitudes, Values, and the Conditions of Learning." In *Advances in the Study of Aggression*, ed. R. J. Blanchard and D. C. Blanchard. Orlando, Fla.: Academic Press, 139–171.

Flavell, J. H. (1986). "The Development of Children's Knowledge about the Appearance-Reality Distinction." *American Psychologist* 41:418–425.

Freud, S. (1930). "*Civilization and its Discontents.*" *Standard Edition* 21:57–145.

_____ (1932). "New Introductory Lectures on Psycho-Analysis." *Standard Edition* 22:1–182.

Gallup, G., Jr., and Newport, F. (1990). "Americans Have Love-Hate Relationship with their TV Sets." *Gallup Poll News Service* 55(21):1–9.

Harris, L. (1977). "Too Much TV Violence." *Harris Survey*, 4 August, 1–2.

Hearold, S. (1986). "A Synthesis of 1043 Effects of Television on Social Behavior." In *Public Communication and Behavior*, vol. 1, ed G. Comstock. Orlando, Fla.: Academic Press, 65–133.

Heller, M. S., and Polsky, S. (1976). *Studies in Violence and Television*. New York: American Broadcasting Company.

Hennigan, K. M., Del Rosario, M. L., Heath, L., et al. (1982). "Impact of the Introduction of Television on Crime in the United States: Empirical Findings and Theoretical Implications." *Journal of Personal and Social Psychology* 42:461–477.

Johnson, J. M., and DeBerry, M. M., Jr. (1990). *Criminal Victimization 1989: A National Crime Survey Report*. Washington, D. C.: U.S. Department of Justice.

Joy, L. A., Kimball, M. M., and Zabrack, M. L. (1986). "Television and Children's Aggressive Behavior." In *The Impact of Television: A Natural Experiment in Three Communities*, ed. T. M. Williams. Orlando, Fla.: Academic Press, 303–360.

Klein, M. (1933). "The Early Development of Conscience in the Child." In *Contributions to Psycho-Analysis 1921–1945*. London: Hogarth Press, 1948, 267–277.

––––– (1934). "On Criminality." In *Contributions to Psycho-Analysis 1921–1945*. London: Hogarth Press, 1948, 278–281.

Kruttschnitt, C., Heath, L., and Ward, D. A. (1986). "Family Violence, Television Viewing Habits, and Other Adolescent Experiences Related to Violent Criminal Behavior." *Criminology* 24:235–267.

Meltzoff, A. N. (1988a). "Infant Imitation After a 1-week Delay: Long-Term Memory for Novel Acts and Multiple Stimuli." *Developmental Psychology* 24:470–476.

––––– (1988b). "Imitation of Televised Models by Infants." *Child Development* 59:1221–1229.

––––– (1992). "Memory in Infancy." In *Encyclopedia of Learning and Memory*, ed. L. R. Squire, J. Byrne, L. Nadel, et al. New York: Macmillan, 271–275.

Meltzoff, A. N., and Moore, M. K. (1983). "Newborn Infants Imitate Adult Facial Gestures." *Child Development* 54:702–709.

––––– (1989). "Imitation in Newborn Infants: Exploring the Range of Gestures Imitated and the Underlying Mechanism." *Developmental Psychology* 25:954–962.

Milavsky, J. R., Kessler, R. C., Stipp, H. H., et al. (1982). *Television and Aggression: A Panel Study*. Orlando, Fla.: Academic Press.

National Center for Health Statistics. (1990). *Vital Statistics of the United States, 1987*. Hyattsville, Md.: U.S. Department of Health and Human Services.

Peter D. Hart Research Associates. (1992). "Would You Give Up TV for a Million Bucks?" *TV Guide* 40, No. 41: 10–17.

Post, S. C., ed. (1972). *Moral Values and the Superego Concept in Psychoanalysis*. New York: International Universities Press.

Rossi, P. H., Waite, E., Bose, C. E., and Berk, R. E. (1974). "The Seriousness of Crimes: Normative Structure and Individual Differences." *American Sociological Review* 39:224–237.

Spitz, R. A. (1958). "On the Genesis of Superego Components." *The Psychoanalytic Study of the Child* 13:375–404.

Wood, W., Wong, F. Y., and Chachere, J. G. (1991). "Effects of Media Violence on Viewers' Aggression in Unconstrained Social Interaction." *Psychological Bulletin* 109:371–383.

World Health Organization. (1989). *World Health Statistics Annual, 1989*. Geneva, Switzerland: World Health Organization.

12

Cultivating and Curing Violence in Children: A Guide to Methods

J. GERALD YOUNG

COLETTE CHILAND

We teach violence to our children. Not all of them, but far too many. Surprisingly, this is refreshing news — because we can stop.

Violence in the world causes deep pessimism and accompanying cynicism about any proposed solutions. This is often reflected in opinions that violent individuals are simply sick, are different because their brains are damaged. In fact, there are no convincing data to support this position. Published scientific research does not give persuasive evidence for brain pathology as a cause of the behavior of a significant percentage of violent individuals. Genetic influences, interacting with environmental molding, may contribute to a temperament that makes *some* individuals more impulsive or more aggressive, but the environment holds the key to violent, aggressive behavior. Individuals who commit violent acts because of brain disorders are relatively rare according to the evidence now available. It is important to recognize them, because they might be repeat offenders and their disorders might be identifiable. However, in order to prevent the development of violent behavior in most children, we have to identify factors other than brain damage.

Children do not arrive in this world as gentle and undemanding creatures. The demanding cries of infants are the biologically necessary assertion of their needs. As they develop into older children it becomes an increasingly complex question whether they are showing "necessary assertion" or disruptive aggression. The struggle with this definition challenges all cultures every day, and all individuals for a lifetime.

Some principles emerge. There are consistent patterns to the therapeutic interventions that prove most useful to children suffering violence, in spite of significant differences in the nature of the violence. Further study of these patterns helps us not only determine the best plans for treatment, but also suggests the types of insults most damaging to children and the timing and nature of interventions most likely to avert the gestation of additional problems in the period following the trauma — in other words, the very phenomena that we should target for our strongest prevention efforts.

What, then, should our prevention efforts focus on? Here we do not consider repeat violent offenders who might occasionally have brain dysfunction. We target the broad indigenous violence that seems so acceptably common in spite of all the protests against it. Some of the sources of the development of violent aggressive behavior in children have become well known.

First, these children have not learned how to manage severely aggressive feelings. Confronted with very intense, impulsive urges to attack someone, they do so. They have not learned the more complex responses involved in inhibiting and deflecting the impulse, postponing it until they have a chance to consider the effects of the impulsive act more fully in their stark reality, and to examine possible alternatives to the violent aggression.

Second, these children have little education concerning their emotions. They are incapable of identifying many of the emotions they experience, fail to understand the events precipitating the emotions, are unfamiliar with the idea of their own internal conflicts as they face common mutually exclusive choices, and lack a reasonable repertoire of coping mechanisms that will help them deflect their most severe aggressive impulses.

Third, abstract education about the behaviors and emotions associated with aggression is insufficient to curb aggressive behaviors in children for whom it has become a pattern. Aggression has become an ingrained response (altering the cellular structure of the brain) that has in some manner solved many of their problems (while creating others). Only structured experiences with alternative circumstances, challenges, and behaviors will be sufficient to enable these children to gradually change their responses. The description of the program in Jerusalem not only makes clear what the components of such a program ought to be, but also suggests the types of problems children face that require a prolonged therapeutic experience.

Fourth, in spite of both educational and therapeutic/ experiential approaches, or the best prevention efforts, violent aggression can be stimulated by chronically noxious influences, such as abuse, poverty, extreme unpredictability in the environment, drug addiction, and other factors. This category among the sources of violent aggression is largely outside the domain of psychiatrists, and related prevention programs lie with the larger political and economic programs that have been progressing over time. While clinicians can target these influences for preventive efforts only in small ways, neglecting them in individual therapeutic efforts can be very damaging. The poverty of a patient might not be subject to amelioration by the clinician, but ignoring the role played by that poverty and the consequent disorganization of a patient's life in stimulating aggression can be very damaging to treatment.

Persistent, flagrant, and unjust political, economic, and legal structures lead to despair and rage. Along the way, individuals (or entire groups) may relinquish respect for and adherence to the law. Every country has examples of these problems, particularly visible in the underclasses. Children grow up knowing that their opportunities for the future are minimal, if they exist at all. Regrettably, even attempts to solve these problems in developed countries lead to other problems. A Brazilian economist said to one of us (JGY) that a lack of equal opportunity in some countries is matched by opportunistic equality in others—to which I added that this often leads to opportunistic inequality, as deeply rooted economic and political success ultimately eludes underprivileged groups who make superficial, opportunistic demands. Once again, these large, complex problems lie outside the scope of psychiatry, but ignorance of their influence undercuts the utility of efforts to reduce violence.

One view of the lack of attention to the problems of children in the United States (nearly 25 percent live in poverty) is that it is "benign neglect": one way or another, a child who has a little motivation (!) has ample opportunity to better himself in this country. We suggest that it might be more accurately described as "neglect of the benign"—they do not vote, lack economic power, and are generally unable to defend themselves. As might be anticipated, however, society pays for this later. The bill is high, particularly because of the violence that is spawned by this neglect.

The violence of natural disasters (earthquakes, hurricanes, floods, etc.) cannot be prevented, but its effects can be reduced. The project in Armenia was conducted along clear, practical lines in a manner that can be repeated elsewhere. Similarly, national political violence is recurrent, and our best hope for preventing later disorders is improved management of children in need in refugee circumstances and other traumatic situations. The multitude of differences in refugee populations has been documented, but so have those elements common to the efforts most likely to substantially reduce the later serious psychological morbidity to which these children are vulnerable. Family and community violence can be approached more directly by clinicians. Here, the work with community police in New Haven and with children witnessing murder of one parent by another in London are important models for minimizing the potentially chronic, serious psychological damage resulting from violence thrust into the lives of children. Certainly we have an increased understanding of how growing up in a family in which one or both parents are alcoholic becomes a stimulation toward violent aggressive behaviors, and this can lead to improved prevention efforts in these families.

It is surprising and revealing to trace the development of legal precedents that reflect individualism and the rights of individuals to defend themselves. These laws reflect a cultural philosophy of a people that has grown up over many years. Similarly, while research methodologists can argue the evidence concerning the effects of violent television programs on a developing child who demonstrates increasingly aggressive behavior, the current research evidence and time spent watching the "graphic" (i.e., shockingly blatant) television episodes combine to make a conclusion obvious. This is a powerful stimulant to violent behavior in later life for children who develop under its influence. While adults passively argue the complexities of the situation, an obvious, easily preventable intense stimulant for violent behavior goes untouched. This is repeated in protracted discussions about "graphic depictions" (bloody, egregious, ruthless, repetitive) of violence in videotapes, videogames, and coming soon on compact disc.

Many questions have been asked in this volume, but most will not be readily answered. The frustrating truth is that their current function is to guide our further efforts to combat the development of violent behaviors in children in the future. If we are to help children cope with aggressive impulses we have to do so within the context of recognizing that aggression is "normal," a predictable, evolutionarily molded, biological set of response capacities within the brain. Aggression can be provoked by known categories of stimuli whose differences influence the nature of the aggression stimulated. This can be a consideration in prevention plans.

This volume began with comments concerning our willingness to accept distorted, contradictory ideas about aggression because of their context. Examples are the willingness of individuals to believe the urgings of dictators or the rationalizations of manufacturers selling games depicting and encouraging graphic violence. How do neighbors transform themselves so that they are able to become violent toward each other? How do individuals overcome their religious beliefs in order to engage in combat-sanctioned killing, and how do nations manage and alter the illegality of killing for the exceptional circumstances of war—requiring not only that killing be permitted, but that individuals be compelled to join the military in order to kill? How is legitimacy for these sociopolitical decisions conferred, and how does the individual recognize the time at which laws are no longer civilized and that one has the responsibility to move against them?

These questions involve the determination of the legitimacy of aggression and violence in differing circumstances, and the criteria for assuring that rebellion is acceptable. Such questions are exceedingly complex, and answers may seem arbitrary at the time they are initially raised because no answer seems fully acceptable—until later, when the matter might seem clear in retrospect. If such questions confuse adults, they illuminate for us how difficult it is for children to learn the myriad rules, differing in place, time, and situation, that guide our judgment that aggressive behavior is or is not appropriate in a given circumstance. At a cultural level, how do we explain the paradoxes of war, of torture, of slavery to children? At a personal level, what do we do to interrupt the vicious cycles of violence begetting violence across generations of families?

Regrettably, intensive scholarly work, the accretion of detailed knowledge about violence, and extensively available facts fail to have much effect on the cultivation of violence in our children.

Something more forceful is necessary. At the least, however, we can feel some accomplishment in the knowledge that our understanding of how violence is cultivated in children—and, on the other hand, how it can be "cured"—has reached a point at which it can guide our decisions.

HOW DO WE CULTIVATE VIOLENCE IN CHILDREN?

Family Methods

1. Teach children that deciding whether to be aggressive or not in a given situation is easy.

2. Do not provide limits to aggressive behavior, for fear that it will encroach upon creativity, self-expression, individuality, or individual rights.

3. When you do provide limits, do so in an arbitrary, severe, righteous fashion, assuring that the child feels intimidated, helpless, and frightened. When particularly well done, it will aggravate others sufficiently that they will suggest that firm limits are the source of the problem.

4. Point to overzealous prohibitions against violence in the past and not only recommend discarding them, but announce that there was never any basis for any rules.

5. Teach children that action and aggression are effective and strong, while language and thought are ineffective and weak.

6. Teach children that there is only one solution to a problem (for a strong person), not many.

7. Teach children that experiencing, thinking about, and talking about feelings is weak. Showing feelings is obviously forbidden.

8. Teach children that if you are "up front" and have told people about your needs and plans, this justifies any behavior—you "have to do your thing."

9. Teach children that they *always* have to stand up for what they want.

10. Teach children that they should *never* stand up for what they want.

11. Explain to children that they are never to hit anyone, but that you have to hit *them* because their behavior is so bad.

12. Explain to children that the reason that you scream so much is that their behavior is so hopeless.

Treatment Methods

13. When a child is exposed to the traumatic effects of natural, political, community, or family violence, provide aid and therapy outside the child's family and familiar community as much as is practical. Use only experts the child has never met, and provide the aid in a distant, neutral setting.

14. When a child is exposed to the traumatic effects of natural, political, community, or family violence, keep experts to the side so that they do not interfere.

15. When 10-year-old, severely aggressive children require treatment, provide them with a one-month treatment program. This will not only be less expensive and more acceptable to third-party payers, but will be sufficient experience for the children to learn that the coping methods they learned in the past month are more reliable than those they depended on for ten years.

16. Promote the point of view that the proper response to very aggressive behavior is always medication, and that behavioral treatments are ineffective.

17. Promote the point of view that medication never has a role in the treatment of aggression.

Cultural Methods

18. Teach children that violent aggression is done by others, who have brain damage, not by ordinary people.

19. Convince the public that parental problems (e.g., alcoholism, drug use, spouse abuse, etc.) have a minimal influence on children, who typically do not notice the problem or do not understand it if they see it.

20. Provide clear models that the only reliable method for adapting to difficulties is through aggressive behavior. This can be achieved particularly forcefully if the models are those a child depends upon, loves, and is close to. If this is not possible, provide

surrogate models through movies, television programs, video-tapes, and videogames. While not as close or emotionally powerful as those within the child's own world, they have the advantages of availability at any time the child chooses, idealization, endless repetition, peer approval, and obvious cultural sanction.

21. Provide advertising commercials that demonstrate the value of abrasively, provocatively aggressive behavior and demean those who are thoughtful or attempt compromise.

22. Encourage the best athletes to promote the idea that intensely aggressive assertion, being "in your face" inside or outside the game, is the key element of athletic (or life) success.

23. Suggest to the public, but especially to children and adolescents, that the amount of stimulation to aggression is immaterial, that people can control themselves and limits are always censorship.

24. Suggest to the public that children are born as placid, undemanding, unaggressive individuals, and that the imposition of discipline and limits to their desires will only cause neurotic guilt.

25. Spread the idea that indulgence of children is a good method for teaching self-control. Encourage the public to recognize that self-gratification inevitably leads to self-control.

26. Spread the idea that severe discipline of children is a good method for teaching self-control.

HOW DO WE "CURE" VIOLENCE IN CHILDREN?

Stop cultivating it.

INDEX